A CourseGuide for

Understanding World Religions

Irving Hexham

ZONDERVAN ACADEMIC

A CourseGuide for Understanding World Religions

Copyright © 2019 by Zondervan

Requests for information should be addressed to:
Zondervan, *3900 Sparks Dr. SE, Grand Rapids, Michigan 49546*

ISBN 978-0-310-11106-1 (softcover)

All Scripture quotations, unless otherwise indicated, are taken from The Holy Bible, New International Version®, NIV®. Copyright © 1973, 1978, 1984, 2011 by Biblica, Inc.® Used by permission of Zondervan. All rights reserved worldwide. www.Zondervan.com. The "NIV" and "New International Version" are trademarks registered in the United States Patent and Trademark Office by Biblica, Inc.®

Any internet addresses (websites, blogs, etc.) and telephone numbers in this book are offered as a resource. They are not intended in any way to be or imply an endorsement by Zondervan, nor does Zondervan vouch for the content of these sites and numbers for the life of this book.

No part of this publication may be reproduced, stored in a retrieval system, or transmitted in any form or by any means — electronic, mechanical, photocopy, recording, or any other — except for brief quotations in printed reviews, without the prior permission of the publisher.

Printed in the United States of America

CONTENTS

Introduction 5

1. Introductory Issues in the Study of Religion 7
2. A Biased Canon 12
3. African Religious Traditions 15
4. Witchcraft and Sorcery 19
5. God in Zulu Religions 22
6. The Case of Isaiah Shembe 26
7. The Origins of Yogic Religions 30
8. The Richness of the Hindu Traditions 34
9. Rethinking the Hindu Tradition 37
10. Gandhi the Great Contrarian 40
11. Buddhism 44
12. The Development of Buddhist Belief and Practice 48
13. The Moral Quest of Edward Conze 52
14. The Other Yogic-Type Traditions 55
15. Early Judaism 59
16. Rabbinic and Other Judaism 63
17. Jewish Faith and Practice 68

4 | Understanding World Religions

18. **Martin Buber's Zionist Spirituality**..........................72
19. **Christianity**..77
20. **Christian History**..82
21. **Christian Faith and Practice**..............................87
22. **Christian Politics according to Abraham Kuyper**..........92
23. **The Challenge of Islam**...................................97
24. **Muslim Beliefs and Practices**............................102
25. **Muslim Piety**..107
26. **Sayyid Qutb and the Rebirth of Contemporary Islam**......111

Introduction

Welcome to *A CourseGuide for Understanding World Religions*. These guides were created for formal and informal students alike who want to engage deeper in biblical, theological, or ministry studies. We hope this guide will provide an opportunity for you to grow not only in your understanding, but also in your faith.

How to Use This Guide

This guide is meant to be used in conjunction with the book *Understanding World Religions* and its corresponding videos, *Understanding World Religions Video Lectures*. After you have read each chapter in the book and watched the accompanying video lesson, the materials in this guide will help you review and assess what you have learned. Application-oriented questions are included as well.

Each CourseGuide has been individually designed to best equip you in your studies, but in general, you can expect the following components. Most CourseGuides begin every chapter with a "You Should Know" section, which highlights key terminology, people, and facts to remember. This section serves as a helpful summary for directing your studies. Reflection questions, typically two to three per chapter, prompt you to summarize key points you've learned. Discussion questions invite you to an even deeper level of engagement. Finally, most chapters will end with a short quiz to test your retention. You can find the answer key to each quiz at the bottom of the page following it.

For Further Study

CourseGuides accompany books and videos from some of the world's top biblical and theological scholars. They may be used independently, or in small groups or classrooms, offering quality instruction to equip students for academic and ministry pursuits. If you would like to engage in further study with Zondervan's CourseGuides, the full lineup may be viewed online. After completing your studies with *A CourseGuide for Understanding World Religions*, we recommend moving on to *A CourseGuide for Seeking Allah, Finding Jesus*; *A CourseGuide for Apologetics at the Cross*; and *A CourseGuide for Evangelism in a Skeptical World*.

CHAPTER 1

Introductory Issues in the Study of Religion

You Should Know

- Émile Durkheim defined religion as "a unified system of beliefs and practice relative to sacred things . . . beliefs and practices which unite into one single moral community called a Church."

- Immanual Kant defined religion as "the recognition of all duties as divine commands."

- Max Müller defined religion as "a body of doctrines handed down by tradition, or in canonical books, and containing all that constitutes the faith of Jew, Christian, or Hindu."

- Stark/Bainbridge defined religion as "human organizations primarily engaged in providing general compensators based on supernatural assumptions"; they later refined the definition to "systems of general compensators based on supernatural assumptions" and spoke of five dimensions of "religiousness": belief, practice, experience, knowledge, and consequences.

- Bultmann defined myth as a story that is simply untrue.

- Eliade/Campbell/Jung defined religion as some sort of special story containing unique insights into religious truth, archaic insights often lost to humans living in industrial societies.

- Smart/Malinowski defined myth as any story which affects the way people live; not necessarily historical or unhistorical, it can be true/false, historical/unhistorical; enables members of different societies to make sense of their lives/world; concerned with the relationship of a people with other peoples/nature/supernatural

- Explicit religion: what people actually believe is determined by what they say

- Implicit religion: what people actually believe is determined by the way they live

Reflection Questions

1. What is religion? What is myth? What is the difference between the two?

2. Why do Tillich and Welbourn argue that religion can't be defined by visible institutions and rituals?

3. If an anthropologist studied your ontological commitments, or "implicit religion," what would he or she find? What if he or she studied your "explicit religion," or creed and practice? Write a paragraph to describe each.

Discussion Question

1. Use Ninian Smart's characteristics of religion to explain why the following are or are not religious acts. For each, list the characteristics of religious acts that are present and the characteristics that are absent:

    – A graduation ceremony

- A Muslim's pilgrimage to Mecca

- A rock concert

- A church service you have attended

Quiz

1. Religion has been defined by scholars as:
   a) "A story that is simply untrue"
   b) "A unified system of beliefs and practices relative to sacred things"
   c) "A story with culturally formative power"
   d) All of the above

2. Which of the following scholars should NOT be associated with religious studies?
   a) Stark
   b) Eliade
   c) Montgomery
   d) Durkheim

3. The actual practices and beliefs of people as discovered by others through careful observation of their actions constitutes:
   a) Explicit religion
   b) Mythical religion
   c) Implicit religion
   d) Traditional religion

4. (T/F) However myth is defined, its success depends on people accepting and acting upon its message.

5. (T/F) Ninian Smart defined religion as a set of institutionalized rituals identified with a tradition.

6. (T/F) Many secular movements appear religious.

7. (T/F) Kant said, "a unified system of beliefs and practice relative to sacred things . . . beliefs and practices which unite into one single moral community called a Church."

8. (T/F) Bultmann said that a myth is a story that is simply untrue.

9. What people actually believe is determined by what they say. This is called:

a) Explicit religion
b) External religion
c) Internal religon
d) Implicit religion

10. What people actually believe is determined by the way they live. This is called:

a) Explicit religion
b) External religion
c) Internal religon
d) Implicit religion

ANSWER KEY

1. B, 2. C, 3. C, 4. T, 5. T, 6. T, 7. F, 8. F, 9. A, 10. D

CHAPTER 2

A Biased Canon

You Should Know

- Recognizing the power of and inclination toward bias is essential in developing the critical thinking necessary in academic work.

- The study of African religions has traditionally suffered from an implicit racist bias.

- Theodore M. Ludwig classifies African religions together with the native religions of Australia, North and South America, Indonesia, the South Pacific, and various other areas where he finds similar patterns of myth and ritual.

- Such church fathers as St. Augustine of Hippo and Tertullian were African and, in all probability, black.

- François-Marie Arouet, known as Voltaire, set the general tone of Enlightenment attitudes to Africans. Although derogatory remarks may be found throughout his work, his short essay "The Negro" outlined his position. He tells his readers, "They are not capable of any great application or association of ideas and seem formed neither of the advantages nor abuses of our philosophy."

- While Jean-Jacques Rousseau is remembered for his attack on slavery, it is forgotten that he also spoke quite freely of "negroes and savages." In fact, when Rousseau's views are examined in detail, his assessment of the "noble savage" mirrors modern racism.

Reflection Questions

1. Use Hexham's examination of Ninian Smart's *The World's Religions* (1989) to create a list of at least five ways bias might appear in a text, or five ways to spot bias.

2. List at least three causes Hexham gives for the neglect of African religions in nineteenth-to-twenty-first-century scholarship.

3. Why might Indian religions have received preferential treatment over African religions by nineteenth-century scholars?

Discussion Question

1. Explain how Africa was described before the Enlightenment and then in light of the Enlightenment, focusing on key people and their ideas about the continent.

Quiz

1. (T/F) All people have biases. Therefore, most of us are very quick to recognize when we see or hear a biased perspective.

2. (T/F) Hexham suggests most textbooks dealing with African religions are racially biased.

3. (T/F) The dearth of articles on African religion in academic journals is a reflection of the lack of scholarship on the topic.

4. (T/F) In his book *The World's Religions*, Ninian Smart treats the diversity of religion in India as an exciting and creative phenomenon, yet dismisses African religious diversity.

5. (T/F) Hexham argues that a good case can be made for the suggestion that modern racism originated in the Enlightenment.

6. The World Congress of Religions took place in:
   a) 1793
   b) 1883
   c) 1893
   d) 1983

7. Smart dismisses rich African mythologies as myths of:
   a) Disorder
   b) Death

c) Tricks
d) All of the above

8. Smart conveys that African religions have a particular problem with:
    a) Ancient myths
    b) Witch doctors
    c) Modern science
    d) All of the above

9. The World Congress of Religions
    a) Described African religions as "religions of fear"
    b) Gave no attention whatsoever to African religions
    c) Described African religions as "elementary"
    d) All of the above

10. Reasons why an appreciation of African religion has not developed include
    a) The unavailability of religious texts containing scriptures of African religions
    b) The reliance of most scholars on written scriptures to interpret a religion
    c) A shortage of white anthropologists/missionaries in visiting Africa
    d) A & B

ANSWER KEY

1. F, 2. T, 3. F, 4. T, 5. T, 6. C, 7. D, 8. C, 9. B, 10. D

CHAPTER 3

African Religious Traditions

You Should Know

- There are many different African religions; therefore, to speak of "African religion" requires certain qualifications.

- Primal religions are identifiable with what Robert Redfield calls "little traditions," where charismatic experiences, healings, prophecies, visions, and so on are the principal concern of devotees. In primal religions shamans or similar ritual figures communicate between this world and the next, often with the aim of placating the ancestors.

- To understand traditional religions, particularly African religions, it is necessary to suspend judgment as to which view of the universe — the secular, traditional, modern Christian, or any other alternative view — is true. We must enter as fully as possible into the perspective of someone living in a traditional society which sees all phenomena as an expression of mysterious power.

- Traditional Africans, such as the Baganda and Zulu peoples, do not make distinctions between the natural and supernatural. This means they do not recognize a distinction between the secular and the sacred. Yet the idea of the "sacred" or "holy" is deeply ingrained in religious studies.

- Traditional Africans describe this power as an all-pervasive psychic force behaving very much like electricity is believed to behave in our society. People and things which are "positively charged" with power can pass it on by contact to anyone who is "negatively charged." Unless this process is properly controlled, damage will result.

- "Great Traditions" or "World Religions": Buddhism, Christianity, Confucianism, Hinduism, Islam, and Judaism
- "Traditional religions:" smaller religious traditions that are usually found in non-Western societies that lack written scriptures, the greatest concentration of which is found in Africa
- "Primal religions": identified by John Taylor because in his view they draw on deep-rooted primal, or basic, experiences common to all humans, experiences capable of being formed into coherent ways of seeing the world; such religions lack written scriptures and recorded histories and often share a belief in evil power identified with sorcery or witchcraft, specialized healers, psychic events, and the importance of ancestors
- Primal experiences: important for African religious movements because they affirm the reality of traditional mythologies and the foundation myths of new religious movements like the amaNazaretha

Reflection Questions

1. Describe the difference between a "sacred-secular distinction" (a concept advanced by some European theorists of religion) and a "hierarchy of power" (a belief system observed in many traditional African societies).

2. Based on your own worldview and belief system, suggest an explanation of primal experiences such as "dreams, visions, voices, spiritual healings, a sense of presence or awe, notions of destiny, [and] sightings of the dead."

3. Write a paragraph describing how power, in the primal worldview, is something like electricity.

Discussion Question

1. Summarize and explain the fundamentals of the African religious traditions described in this session.

Quiz

1. (T/F) There are very few African religious traditions; therefore, it is possible to speak about "African religion" without qualification.

2. (T/F) African traditional religions, like most grassroots religious movements, are based on the religious experience of their founders and members.

3. (T/F) To understand traditional religions, particularly African religions, it is necessary to suspend judgment as to which view of the universe is true.

4. (T/F) It is not necessary to suspend the Western belief that the "natural" and "supernatural" are separate spheres in order to understand the traditional experience of traditional Africans.

5. (T/F) Traditional African understanding of power should be viewed in much the same way as we understand electricity to function in our society.

6. Small religious traditions that lack written scriptures and are usually found in non-Western societies are sometimes called _____ religions.
   a) Ancestral
   b) Original
   c) Primal
   d) Primate

7. African religious traditions share many common features that can be considered a worldview that may be identified as the _____.
   a) Ancestral vision
   b) Original vision
   c) Primal vision
   d) Primate vision

8. Ritual figures that communicate between this world and the next, often with the goal of placating ancestors, are known as _____.
   a) Priests
   b) Shamans

c) Imams
  d) Prophets

9. To properly study and better understand African religions in a meaningful way, we must move beyond the mere analysis of written texts to comprehend the real-life _____ of living peoples.

  a) Interpretations
  b) Beliefs
  c) Practices
  d) Experiences

10. Power is sometimes personalized in African religion by taking on the form of a river or animal, or it can be inherent and punish people by bringing what we might call _____.

  a) Karma
  b) Bad luck
  c) Reincarnation
  d) Mojo

ANSWER KEY

1. F, 2. T, 3. T, 4. F, 5. T, 6. C, 7. C, 8. B, 9. D, 10. B

CHAPTER 4

Witchcraft and Sorcery

You Should Know

- The discussion of witchcraft in this chapter does not refer to Wicca, various new religions that claim members belong to an ancient pre-Christian faith, or even to modern witches; it is about traditional witchcraft in Africa clearly believed to be evil by members of the societies where it occurs.

- Belief in traditional witches and witchcraft arises naturally from the structure of traditional African beliefs.

- Whereas witchcraft is psychic in nature, sorcery involves use of material objects.

- The powers used by sorcerers are usually used for evil purposes, but they can be used for good, just as the powers of healers may also be used for evil.

- Despite what they may think or claim, Westerners also believe in a psychic reality as demonstrated by our use of terminology such as "luck" or "fate."

- In African societies ancestral ghosts are often regarded as agents of disease.

- The "evil eye" is another psychic cause of disease according to African religions.

- Sorcerers: specialists who have learned their trade by apprenticeship to another sorcerer or through a direct call from a spirit

Reflection Questions

1. Compare and contrast witchcraft and sorcery, then compare and contrast curses and evil eye.

2. How would you describe the relationship of "personal or supernatural causes" and "impersonal or natural causes" in your own worldview? Does every event have both an impersonal and a personal cause? Does every event fall in one category or the other? Explain your perspective.

3. Even if a woman from a traditional African society believes that a mosquito's bite caused her child's malaria, why might she not believe that a visit to a medical doctor is a sufficient response?

Discussion Question

1. Summarize and explain traditional African beliefs about witchcraft, particularly psychic forces and the calling of a diviner.

Quiz

1. (T/F) As used in this chapter, the term "witchcraft" always refers to Wicca.

2. (T/F) Witchcraft always involves the use of material objects.

3. (T/F) Sorcery is psychic in nature.

4. (T/F) In African societies ancestral ghosts are often regarded as agents of disease.

5. (T/F) The "evil eye" is another psychic cause of disease according to African religions.

6. Under _____ and other forms of colonial rule in Africa, the practice of witchcraft and bad sorcery was made illegal.
   a) British
   b) American

c) French
d) Indian

7. Some writers suggest that however much witchcraft and sorcery may have been feared in African religions, they nevertheless served a definite _____ function.

a) Religious
b) Theological
c) Social
d) Economic

8. _____ societies tend to think in terms of invisible electrical forces, while people in traditional societies think in terms of psychic forces such as witchcraft and sorcery.

a) Eastern
b) Western
c) African
d) Chinese

9. Rather than viewing African religions as "_____," we need to view them in comparison with similar traditions in our own society.

a) Valid
b) Tolerable
c) Strange
d) Right

10. Many charismatic Christians in the West suggest that routine illnesses can be caused by _____. Thus, there is a logic to the beliefs of traditional societies that is not very different from the logic of certain religious groups in the West.

a) Karma
b) God
c) Angels
d) Evil spirits

ANSWER KEY

1. F, 2. F, 3. F, 4. T, 5. T, 6. A, 7. C, 8. B, 9. C, 10. D

CHAPTER 5

God in Zulu Religions

You Should Know

- Scholars of African religions argue that traditional African beliefs assume the notion of a High God. Hexham argues that this view does not square with the available evidence.

- Many African and other traditional, or primal, religions appear to lack any awareness of God or, in some cases, even gods. Nevertheless, such peoples had religions of their own and quickly accepted the existence of God once Christian or Muslim beliefs were presented to them.

- European slave traders claimed that Africans lacked souls, were lower on the evolutionary scale, and therefore were not fully human. Although most Christians rejected these assertions, the views nevertheless had a profound effect on how Africans were viewed. Many Christians argued that if Africans could comprehend Christian theology it was proof that they had souls; thus, they insisted, Africans shared a belief in a High God.

- Hexham traces the development of the idea of "Unkulunkulu" among the Zulus of South Africa to seriously challenge the claim that African religions affirmed a High God.

- Ludwig Wittgenstein said, "The word 'God' is amongst the earliest learnt . . . The word is used like a word representing a person . . . If the question arises as to the existence of a god or God, it plays an entirely different role to that of the exis-tence of any person or object I ever heard of. One said, *had to say* [italics mine], that one *believed* in the existence, and if one did not believe, this was regarded as something bad."

- Zulu beliefs and practices were challenged by the arrival of Europeans and their "strange" beliefs, but within several generations an adaptation had taken place which enabled Zulus to deal with the Europeans on their own terms.

- Unkulunkulu: the Creator of First Cause, according to Zulu belief

- Lord of Heaven: Zulu belief in a sky deity

- Henry Callaway: His book *The Religious System of the Amazulu* (1870) is one of our main sources for information about Zulu religion as practiced by traditional Zulu in the nineteenth century, and a pioneer missionary who was remarkably sympathetic to African views of religion and African spirituality.

Reflection Questions

1. From the widespread use of Henry Callaway's writing to support the idea of Zulu belief in Unkulunkulu as a high God, what do we learn are potential dangers in scholarship and in the observation of other cultures?

2. What does Hexham suggest may have been the origin of the idea of a 'Lord of Heaven' among the Zulu?

3. From the history of Zulu contact with Europeans, what can you learn about sharing your own faith with people of a completely different religious tradition and worldview?

Discussion Question

1. African peoples had religions of their own and quickly accepted the existence of God once Christian or Muslim beliefs were presented to them. To illustrate this process and the way African religions may not include an awareness of God, explain the case of traditional Zulu beliefs. How does it illustrate the way people learn to use the word "God"?

Quiz

1. Most scholars of African religions argue that traditional African beliefs assume the notion of
    a) Transcendence
    b) Immutability
    c) A High God
    d) A plurality of gods

2. The claim that Africans lacked souls, were lower on the evolutionary scale, and therefore not fully human was advanced by European
    a) Scientists
    b) Slave traders
    c) Missionaries
    d) B & C

3. Hexham traces the development of the idea of _____ among the Zulus of South Africa to seriously challenge the claim that African religions affirmed a High God.
    a) Unlukunluku
    b) Coca-Cola
    c) Unkul Kulu
    d) Unkulunkulu

4. Although Christianity has historically disapproved of and inspired anti-_____ movements, by the time a powerful anti-_____ lobby developed in the late eighteenth century, European slavers argued that _____ was justified.
    a) Cosmetics
    b) Evil spirits
    c) Slavery
    d) All of the above

5. A key source documenting Zulu belief in a sky deity is the published work of
    a) Henry Callaway
    b) Eli Callaway
    c) Emile Durkheim
    d) None of the above

6. Eventually, in the study of African religions, a norm developed that however different traditional African religions might be from the great religious traditions, they all shared a belief in at least a distant
   a) Great Spirit
   b) High God
   c) Warrior God
   d) Ultimate Deity

7. The truth is that many African and other traditional or primal religions appear to lack any awareness whatsoever of
   a) A written scripture
   b) God/gods
   c) The Holy Spirit
   d) All of the above

8. White Europeans were similar to "Unkulunkulu" for the Zulus because they too brought advances in
   a) Technology
   b) Foreign currency
   c) Peace
   d) B & C

9. The picture of Zulu religion derived from the earliest period of recorded contact between Zulu and European cultures (1836–37) is of an essentially _____ society.
   a) Agrarian
   b) Nomadic
   c) Militant
   d) Secular

10. Many missionaries eventually confirmed that the closest the Zulu demonstrated to having any kind of understanding of God was essentially a rudimentary form of
    a) Sorcery
    b) Ancestor worship
    c) Wicca
    d) Humanism

ANSWER KEY

1. C, 2. B, 3. D, 4. C, 5. A, 6. B, 7. B, 8. A, 9. D, 10. B

CHAPTER 6

The Case of Isaiah Shembe

You Should Know

- One of the justifications for African slavery was to claim that Africans were not truly human because they lacked a soul. This argument was developed on the basis of supposed observations of African life showing that Africans, unlike the Chinese and Indians, had failed to develop anything like Buddhism or Hinduism and that African society lacked all manifestations of religion.

- Until the 1980s the "Independent Church" movements were widely regarded as deviant social groups motivated more by politics than by religion.

- G. C. Oosthuizen argued that groups such as Shembe's amaNazarites needed to be viewed "in the context of Zulu" religion; Shembe, then, was seen by his followers as "the manifestation of God."

- Bengt Sundkler countered that Oosthuizen was imposing European standards on the Africans and misunderstood Zulu language and idioms.

- If we are serious about studying the full spectrum of religion, and not just tidy traditions with long-established scriptures, we need to incorporate anthropological methods to allow us to engage in the empirical study of living religions.

- Isaiah Shembe: arguably the most famous founder of an African Independent Church in the whole of Africa

- The amaNazarites: the main modern religion founded by the Zulu religious leader Isaiah Shembe

- *Prester John*: a bestselling novel by John Buchan that vividly illustrates popular attitudes toward African religious movements early in the twentieth century

- G. C. Oosthuizen: attempted a new interpretation of African Independent Churches in his controversial book *The Theology of a South African Messiah*

- Absolom Vilakazi: In his book, *Shembe: The Revitalization of African Society*, he explicitly claimed that Oosthuizen misunderstood both the Zulu language and its numerous idioms, as well as the African Christian Churches.

Reflection Questions

1. How does the conflict between Sundkler/Vilakazi and Oosthuizen illustrate a) the importance of describing one's methods of research, and b) the danger of trusting a scholar based solely upon his/her ethnicity or religious background?

2. According to Londa Shembe, are the amaNazarites a Christian denomination? Why, does Hexham say, is it impossible to correctly describe amaNazarite religion by studying its published texts?

3. How did Lomba Shembe and Amos Shembe's visions for the future of the amaNazaretha differ?

Discussion Question

1. This session deals with some problems encountered by scholars who attempt to study primal religions. What are those problems, especially as it relates to the major scholarly literature and some traditions surrounding perceptions of the Zulu religious leader Isaiah Shembe?

Quiz

1. (T/F) Isaiah Shembe is arguably the most famous founder of an African Independent Church in the whole of Africa.

2. (T/F) "Independent Church" movements were widely regarded as deviant social groups motivated more by politics than by religion until just before World War II.

3. (T/F) The argument that Africans were not truly human was developed by claiming they had failed to develop anything like Buddhism or Hinduism and lacked all manifestations of religion.

4. (T/F) If Africans lacked religion, it was argued, they must not have a soul and were therefore not fully human.

5. (T/F) An essentially hostile attitude remains toward African Independent Church movements such as that reflected in John Buchan's best-selling novel *Call of the Wild* (1910..

6. Isaiah Shembe's followers were known as
   a) Shembeans
   b) AmaNazarites
   c) Zulus
   d) Independents

7. African Independent Churches and other religious movements were initially called
   a) Indigenous
   b) Ethiopian
   c) Nationalist
   d) A & C

8. British missionary leaders argued that African religious movements, unlike "true Christian churches," did not convert the heathen but led Christians astray by
   a) Teaching them to dance
   b) Encouraging them to pursue hedonism
   c) Condoning witchcraft and polygamy
   d) All of the above

9. G. C. Oosthuizen's work on African Independent Churches reflected a style that was actually more dependent on informants than on
   a) Archaeological digs
   b) Analyzing native dialects

c) Written documents
d) A & B

10. The majority of religious studies scholars concentrate on religions of the written word. In attempting to study African religions that are of a primal orientation, however, we face a different task since they are primarily based upon

   a) Dynamic oral traditions
   b) Complex myths and allegories
   c) Secretive rituals
   d) A & C

ANSWER KEY

1. T, 2. F, 3. T, 4. T, 5. F, 6. B, 7. B, 8. C, 9. C, 10. A

CHAPTER 7

The Origins of Yogic Religions

- Although Muslim rulers and the British after them called the non-Muslim inhabitants of the Indian subcontinent "Hindus" and the term "Hinduism" began to be used to describe the religion of indigenous peoples, the terms "Hinduism" and "Hindus" as related to religion in India have been the source of much dispute.

- Most religious studies textbooks now use terms such as "the Hindu religious tradition" to identify the religions of India. It is important to note, however, that in India itself the terms "Hindu" and "Hinduism" are increasingly used by most Indians to refer to their own religious beliefs and practices.

- The historical background of India as advanced by the great nineteenth-century scholar Max Müller, who claimed Indian religious history began around the middle of the second millennium BC, still dominates scholarship today.

- Müller taught that Indo-European-speaking peoples known as Aryans invaded India from the Northwest and their exploits were reflected in religious texts, the most important of which was the *Rig Veda*, the earliest scripture of the Hindu tradition.

- The Aryan focus on sacrifice was gradually replaced by an increasing interest in metaphysical realities that included intense personal devotion to individual gods.

- Indian subcontinent: roughly divided into three geographic regions, including Himalaya Mountains in the north that separates India from Central Asia, and two vast plains irrigated by the Indus and Ganges rivers and separated by the Vindhya Mountains below the Himalayas

- "Hinduism": connotes a unified religious system which never really existed
- Jawaharlal Nehru: became prime minister of India and argued in his book *The Discovery of India* that words like "Hindu" and "Hinduism" ought to be discarded in favor of the word "Hindi"
- Radhakrishnan: a philosopher who became the vice-president of India and argued in his book *The Hindu View of Life* that "Hindu" actually referred to a particular territory and not a religion

Reflection Questions

1. Describe three evidences that the Aryan invasion thesis may be a false version of India's history.

2. Hexham proposes that we imagine a potential false future interpretation (the theory that Europe was invaded by technologically superior Asians who were followers of Islam) of our own era's shifts in philosophy and demographics. Think about recent changes in your own country and imagine a false explanation that could be proposed by scholars and archaeologists many centuries into the future. How might they explain the changes you've seen?

Discussion Question

1. What are the historical origins of "Hinduism"? Explain why the phrase "the Hindu religious tradition" has largely replaced the term "Hinduism" as a descriptor of the religious traditions of India.

Quiz

1. The historical background of India as advanced by the great nineteenth century scholar _____, who claimed Indian religious history began around the middle of the second millennium BC, still dominates scholarship today.
   a) Gregory L. Possehl
   b) Max Müller

c) Adolf Hittler
d) Max Weber

2. He taught that Indo-European-speaking peoples known as _____ invaded India from the northwest.
   a) Aryans
   b) Europeans
   c) Saxons
   d) Anglos

3. Their exploits were recorded in religious texts, including the earliest and most important scripture of the Hindu tradition known as the _____.
   a) Rig Veda
   b) Bhagavad Gita
   c) Bhagavad Vita
   d) Riv Geda

4. Though most Indians within India use this term to refer to their own religious beliefs/practices, since the early 1970s the term "_____" has gradually fallen into disuse among many scholars in Britain and North America.
   a) Sufism
   b) Christianity
   c) Islam
   d) Hinduism

5. "_____" is now a more popular designation to identify the religions of the Indian subcontinent.
   a) The Christian religious tradition
   b) The Sufi religious tradition
   c) The Islamic religious tradition
   d) The Hindu religious tradition

6. In the 1920s significant attention was given to what became known as the _____ which appeared to provide a context to the earliest scripture of the Hindu tradition.
   a) Aryan Valley civilization
   b) Indian Valley civilization

c) Indus Valley civilization
   d) Indigenous Valley civilization

7. Following the Aryan era in India, a new, world-renouncing religion came into being in India that saw all things as part of an original being or essence. This being was known as

   a) Upanishad
   b) Brahman
   c) Veda
   d) Karma

8. This religion taught that life is a series of rebirths and the aim of religion is to break the bonds of karma and enter into union with either God or the gods, or to be absorbed into the

   a) Essence
   b) Heavens
   c) Void
   d) All of the above

9. Indian religious history changed decisively when _____ invaders began a series of incursions in the eighth century AD, leading to the conquest of northern India.

   a) Barbarian
   b) Chinese
   c) Tibetan
   d) Islamic

10. The Hindu practice whereby a widow was expected to accompany her husband to the grave is known as

    a) Goatee
    b) Suttee
    c) Settee
    d) Hindi

ANSWER KEY

1. B, 2. A, 3. A, 4. D, 5. D, 6. C, 7. B, 8. C, 9. D, 10. B

CHAPTER 8

The Richness of the Hindu Traditions

- The literature of the Hindu tradition is Veda, literally meaning *knowledge*. Hinduism has four main collections of Vedas: *Rig Veda*, *Sama Veda*, *Yajur Veda*, *Atharva Veda*. Each Veda contains various types of text: *Samhitas* are collections of hymns; *Brahmanas* are ritual treaties; *Aranyakas* are forest writings; *Upanishads* are the instructions of a teacher.

- For Hindus the Vedas are sacred texts and the basis of all Indian philosophical thought; unlike the Bible, however, they are rarely read or studied by anyone other than ritual specialists and students in Western countries.

- The sounds associated with the various Vedas and their repetition are more important to Hindus than is their study; this is because reciting the Vedas is believed to have cosmic significance.

- Not all Brahmins perform the religious function of preserving the purity of the Vedas, but only Brahmins are considered worthy of such honors. The Brahmins as a group are the true custodians of the Hindu religious tradition and its texts.

- As sacred texts, the Vedas are considered by most Hindus to be a revelation and, as such, authoritative. Exactly what is meant by revelation in the Hindu tradition is a matter of dispute.

- Through the centuries numerous modes of interpreting the texts and expounding the meanings of the Vedas emerged. These interpretations originated in the great epic poems of the *Ramayana* and the *Mahabharata*.

- Brahmins: an exclusive class, or caste, whose duty it is to preserve the purity of the Vedas and repeat them from memory on ritual occasions
- *Bhagavad Gita*: regarded by many as the most important of all Hindu religious books, it was written around AD 300 and tells the story of the interaction of Prince Arjuna with his charioteer, who, unknown to him, is actually a manifestation of the god Krishna
- Atman: the divine within the human, also frequently described as the human soul
- Brahman: the ultimate divine being, also described as God

Reflection Questions

1. Compare and contrast the view and function of Vedas in Hinduism with the view and function of sacred texts in your own religious tradition.

2. Describe some of the manifestations of Hindu piety. Why might these vary widely from caste to caste, region to region, and family to family?

3. How is a Hindu god's appearance on earth as an avatar different from the historic Christian doctrine of Jesus's incarnation? What other differences do you see between Hindu religious tradition/history and Christian religious tradition/history?

Discussion Question

1. Summarize and explain the Hindu epic literature.

Quiz

1. (T/F) For Hindus the Vedas are sacred texts and the basis of all Indian philosophical thought.

2. (T/F) The meaning of "Veda" is knowledge.

3. (T/F) Hinduism has six main collections of Vedas.

4. (T/F) As many devout Christians with the Bible, the Vedas are frequently read and studied by committed Hindus.

5. (T/F) Probably the most important feature of the Vedas for social life is the division of society into four classes or castes.

6. The collection of Vedas that is known as the instructions of a teacher/teachers is called
    a) *Diwali*
    b) *Mahabharata*
    c) *Upanishads*
    d) *Yoga*

7. The shortest of the Hindu epics is the
    a) *Ramayana*
    b) *Mahabharata*
    c) *Bhagavad Gita*
    d) None of the above

8. The other great Hindu epic is the
    a) *Ramayana*
    b) *Mahabharata*
    c) *Bhagavad Gita*
    d) None of the above

9. The best-known text in Indian literature, regarded by many including Gandhi as the most important of all Hindu religious books, is
    a) *Hare Krishna*
    b) *Bhagavad Gita*
    c) *Brahmanas*
    d) *Qur'an*

10. _____ is the belief that all things are embraced by a universal law of cause and effect that stretches through time.
    a) Samsara
    b) Smri
    c) Shiva
    d) Karma

ANSWER KEY

1. T, 2. T, 3. F, 4. F, 5. T, 6. C, 7. A, 8. B, 9. B, 10. D

CHAPTER 9

Rethinking the Hindu Tradition

You Should Know

- Archaeological discoveries and new thinking about the Aryans have led to a radical revision of the way many educated Hindus understand their own religious tradition.

- Chaudhuri, in his popular if controversial work *Hinduism: A Religion to Live By*, challenges existing ideas about Hinduism's origins maintaining we simply lack fixed archaeological points with which to date documents like the *Rig Veda* and *Bhagavad Gita*, therefore the entire field is open to speculation.

- Lacking firm external evidence or extant texts that can be accurately dated, many scholars turn to a comparative-religion approach to date Hindu literature. The German writer and critic Johann Wolfgang von Goethe (1749–1832) introduced a method of dating literature based on the supposed dates at which certain ideas became popular, yet even this method has not proven to be foolproof; Hindu religious traditions overlap and do not fall into neat evolutionary categories.

- The Ganges River, where numerous temples are now found, plays an important role in Hinduism.

- Hare Krishna is likely the most familiar form of Hinduism among North Americans.

- Different movements within Hinduism are not as definitive as the eleventh-century breach between Eastern Orthodoxy and Roman Catholicism during medieval Christianity.

- There isn't anything in the history of Hinduism that is similar to the Protestant Reformation.
- Hindus have a rich mythology about gods like Shiva, Kali, and Vishnu.

Reflection Questions

1. How do realities of Hindu culture illustrate the inaccuracy of simple evolutionary or progressive theories of the development of the Hindu tradition?

2. Explain the development of classical Hinduism.

3. What similarities to your own system of belief do you find in Hexham's descriptions of the visions of the six schools of Hindu philosophy? What differences strike you?

Discussion Question

1. Compare and contrast the six orthodox schools of Hindu philosophy.

Quiz

1. (T/F) Archaeological discoveries and new thinking about the Aryans have led to a radical revision of the way many educated Hindus understand their own religious tradition.

2. (T/F) Most classical Hindu texts are written in Chinese.

3. (T/F) We know very little about Hinduism before the ninth century AD.

4. (T/F) The Ganges River, where numerous temples are now found, plays an important role in Hinduism.

5. (T/F) Hare Krishna is likely the most familiar form of Hinduism among North Americans.

Rethinking the Hindu Tradition | 39

6. (T/F) Different movements within Hinduism are not as definitive as the eleventh-century breach between Eastern Orthodoxy and Roman Catholicism during medieval Christianity.

7. (T/F) There isn't anything in the history of Hinduism that is similar to the Protestant Reformation.

8. (T/F) Perhaps the best-known Hindu school of philosophy in the Western world is Prabhupada.

9. (T/F) Hindus have a rich mythology about gods like Shiva, Kali, and Vishnu.

10. (T/F) Radhakrishnan was one of the great Hindu reformers who founded the Aryan Society in 1875.

ANSWER KEY

1. T, 2. F, 3. F, 4. T, 5. T, 6. T, 7. T, 8. F, 9. T, 10. F

CHAPTER 10

Gandhi the Great Contrarian

You Should Know

- Married at thirteen, Gandhi and his uneducated wife had several children. His family wanted him to become a barrister, the top legal position in the British system before becoming a judge; Gandhi was an indifferent student in his early years, however. Nevertheless, in September 1888 he went to London to study law at University College, where he encountered both the Vegetarian Society and the Theosophical Society. He began reading the *Bhagavad Gita* and the Christian scriptures.

- He returned to India in 1891 to practice law in Mumbai (then Bombay) but failed to make a success of his new venture. After teaching for a period while continuing his law practice, he accepted a post in Durban, South Africa, in 1893 and soon established a thriving law firm, working in Johannesburg and Durban.

- Tradition claims that while traveling to Pretoria by train one day, Gandhi was thrown out of his first-class compartment by an uncouth railway porter in Pietermaritzburg. He spent a very cold night shivering in an unheated waiting room; the traumatic experience sparked his abiding passion for social justice and developed his philosophy of nonviolence.

- In 1913, Gandhi met Anglican clergyman and social activist Charles Freer Andrews, who was visiting South Africa from India. Andrews was impressed by Gandhi's philosophy and what he saw as his deeply Christian vision, and subsequently persuaded Gandhi to return to India in 1915. Back in India, Gandhi further developed and promoted his views on nonviolence and used such to great effect against British rulers, helping effect India's independence in 1948. A few months later he was murdered by a Hindu fanatic who thought Gandhi was too liberal and therefore not a true Hindu.

- Gandhi argued that the British Empire represented "Satanism," adding, "and they who love God can afford to have no love for Satan." As an empire, he said, it "certainly has been guilty of misdeeds" and "terrible atrocities," while the British government in India was best compared "to a robber."

- Gandhi left behind hundreds of books and articles and a rich political tradition of employing nonviolence to achieve social reform.

- Mohandas (Mahatma) Gandhi: the father of modern India, whose parents were devout Hindus, his mother being particularly pietistic and devoted to the worship of the supreme god, Vishnu. The young Gandhi was also surrounded by people of other faiths, including Jains, whose piety and commitment to nonviolence and vegetarianism impressed him.

- Instead of simply criticizing religious people who engaged in politics as fools or fanatics, Gandhi tried sincerely to understand their viewpoint and judge them in their own terms. He read the great works of philosophy and theology alongside the main scriptures of major world religions.

- "The White Man's Burden": a once-popular poem written by Rudyard Kipling as a comment on the occupation of the Philippines by the U.S

Reflection Questions

1. Hexham describes Gandhi's desire to "improve the object criticized" through criticism, as well as his willingness to look beyond labels to see intent. Do you see these qualities reflected in contemporary interchanges on religious and social questions? If so, how and where do you see them, and if not, how would these qualities change the conversations?

2. In this session, Hexham attempts to apply Gandhi's concerns and perspectives to his own local and national context, in twenty-first-century Canada. Choose some of Gandhi's views as expressed in this chapter and apply them to your local and national context, explaining how Gandhi might constructively criticize your actions or those of your society/government.

3. How did Gandhi interact with "religious people who engaged in politics"? Why?

Discussion Question

1. Explain Gandhi's affinity with Rudyard Kipling and his poem, and how it appealed to him in terms of his own outlook in various ways.

Quiz

1. Mahatma Gandhi's chosen vocation was
    a) Teacher
    b) Lawyer
    c) Priest
    d) Journalist

2. He studied at University College in
    a) Amsterdam
    b) Johannesburg
    c) London
    d) New Delhi

3. What traumatic experience sparked his abiding passion for social justice and developed his philosophy of nonviolence?
    a) His father's murder by militant Muslims when Gandhi was a child
    b) The hungry orphans he saw in India's large cities
    c) A paper he wrote while studying at University College
    d) His experience of being thrown out of his first-class compartment by a railway porter in South Africa

4. In 1913, Gandhi met Anglican clergyman and social activist, Charles Freer Andrews, who was visiting South Africa from

   a) India
   b) Britain
   c) Germany
   d) the United States

5. Hexham claims Gandhi should be remembered as a great

   a) Libertarian
   b) Social activist
   c) Contrarian
   d) Humanitarian

6. (T/F) Gandhi particularly appreciated the works of the famous Anglo-Indian poet William Butler Yeats.

7. (T/F) Gandhi defended the once-popular poem "The White Man's Burden" by arguing that it had "been very much misunderstood."

8. (T/F) In Gandhi's view, Kipling was a racist.

9. (T/F) Gandhi maintained it was racist white colonists who were the real enemies of the British Empire.

10. (T/F) For Gandhi, the idea that individuals would sacrifice themselves for the good of other people in an empire was an acceptable notion.

ANSWER KEY

1. B, 2. C, 3. D, 4. A, 5. C, 6. F, 7. T, 8. F, 9. T, 10. T

CHAPTER 11

Buddhism

You Should Know

- Of all the world's religions, Buddhism is arguably the most misunderstood in Western society. This is the direct result of the work of nineteenth-century European writers who embraced Buddhism as an alternative to Christianity; yet most were agnostics.

- The most successful promoter of Buddhism in the nineteenth century was Sir Edwin Arnold (1832–1904), a liberal Christian, whose poem *The Light of Asia* (1879) became an instant best seller in Britain and America before being translated into numerous other languages. It purports to be a retelling of the life of the Buddha based on original texts, but actually draws on several early English translations of Buddhist scriptures.

- Arnold unashamedly adapted Buddhism and Buddhist texts to what he saw as the interests of his readers; only those elements of the original which could be readily interpreted within a modern mechanistic worldview entered his fascinating yet deeply flawed text.

- Nevertheless, the book was a stunning success and led to tours of Eastern lands and instant acclaim by respected members of indigenous Buddhist groups. However, in terms of accurately conveying Buddhist thought to the West, Arnold actually set things on a very distorted path.

- The great twentieth-century Buddhist scholar and disciple, Edward Conze (1904–1979), lamented that people inspired by Arnold had purged Buddhism of much of its original essence. His classic *Buddhism: Its Essence and Development* insists on viewing Buddhism as it is seen by Buddhists and not as we would like the religion to be.

- Buddhists believe the last words of the Buddha were, "All things are conditional and transient; try to attain your salvation with diligence."

- Siddhartha Gautama: the name of the Buddha who lived sometime in the fifth and sixth centuries BC, probably between 563 and 483, to whose teachings Buddhism is traced

- "Great Renunciation": an act undertaken by Siddhartha of wrenching himself free from his family and normal social commitments

- Two groups within the Buddhist movement: the Hinayana and the Mahayana, also known as the lesser and the greater vehicles

Reflection Questions

1. How did Sir Edwin Arnold choose the texts he would include in his *The Light of Asia*? What do you learn from this about how to gauge an author's credibility?

2. Compare and contrast the Buddhist idea of enlightenment, or salvation, with the idea of salvation in Christianity. In each tradition, how is it attained? Who may attain it? What is it?

3. In a timeline, chart, or paragraph, summarize the rise, spread, and decline of Buddhism throughout India, Central Asia, Eastern Asia, and the West. Include proposed causes for these developments.

Discussion Question

1. Summarize and describe the story of the Buddha, as well as his central teachings.

Quiz

1. Hexham argues that of all the world's religions, Buddhism is arguably the most misunderstood
    a) In Western society
    b) By scholars of religious studies

c) Because its scriptures are so confusing
d) All of the above

2. The most successful promoter of Buddhism in the nineteenth century was

   a) Godfried Lenz
   b) King Ashoka
   c) Sir Edwin Arnold
   d) Edward Conze

3. The twentieth-century Buddhist scholar and disciple _____ _____ lamented that previous scholars had purged Buddhism of much of its original essence.

   a) Sir Edwin Arnold
   b) Edward Conze
   c) Rudyard Kipling
   d) Siddhartha Gautama

4. Buddhism traces its origins back to a teacher known as the Buddha who lived sometime in the

   a) Fifth and sixth centuries AD
   b) Third century BC
   c) Fifth and sixth centuries BC
   d) Time when Christ was on earth

5. Among the many legends surrounding the origins of Buddhism is the story of the Buddha's mother's dream in which a _____ _____ appeared, circled her several times, and then miraculously entered her womb through her side.

   a) White dove
   b) White swallow
   c) Sparrow hawk
   d) White elephant

6. Buddhist tradition maintains that while out riding one day, Siddhartha Gautama (the Buddha) encountered in rapid succession a young child full of energy and joy, a decrepit old man in great pain, a very sick younger man near death, and

a) A funeral procession carrying a decaying corpse
b) A baby white elephant
c) A group of holy men practicing arduous meditation
d) A poem entitled "The Light of Asia"

7. (T/F) After brooding over the significance of the encounters mentioned in number 6, Siddhartha made a momentous decision to leave his home, abandon his family, and seek spiritual truth.

8. (T/F) This began a sixteen-year period of wandering during which he visited numerous sages and holy men.

9. (T/F) After the Buddha's death around 483 BC, his disciples held a great council where they formulated an authoritative canon and established the rules for the order of churches.

10. (T/F) A schism later divided the movement into two groups, the Hinayanists and the Mahayanists.

ANSWER KEY
1. A, 2. C, 3. B, 4. C, 5. D, 6. A, 7. T, 8. F, 9. F, 10. T

CHAPTER 12

The Development of Buddhist Belief and Practice

You Should Know

- Buddhist history may be divided into five-hundred-year periods, a division that is actually preferred by Buddhist scholars since at least the first century AD. Essentially, this approach suggests that the entire universe is in decline; the beginning of the Buddhist era marked a relative high point from which everything gradually degenerates.

- The historical facts regarding the first history of Buddhism in India are scarce and highly debatable. We actually know very little about early Buddhism or what the Buddha taught; all we know is what later generations said he taught.

- Throughout Buddhism's 2500-year history certain realities have characterized its growth, giving rise to a remarkably unified Buddhist ethos with an organic structure:
    - monastic organization upon which everything else is based
    - a series of mediatory practices accompany the growth of Buddhist communities
    - the ultimate goal is the death of individuality or "the extinction of self"

- For the Buddhist, whether this self is a living soul or simply a being who has some sort of individualized existence does not really matter, because God does not exist, and the soul or any form of self or personal identity is an illusion.

- For the vast majority of Buddhists there is neither a self nor a person. All that exists in terms of the human being are a series of sense impressions that can be analyzed with great precision.

- Buddhism is both a highly philosophical and an ultimately experiential religious system of spiritual practices. Central to these practices and beliefs are the four Noble Truths.

- The Buddha was seen not just as a man, nor as a god, but rather as an extraordinary being who brings enlightenment to other sentient beings. The full development of this doctrine of the Buddha, his various manifestations, and his supernatural body took centuries.

- Arhat: a being who earned his or her own individual salvation

- "Dharma" has various meanings in Buddhism: that which represents the whole of reality; true reality versus the world of illusion; the teachings of the Buddha; his doctrines/sutras/writings/truths; actions by human beings (similar to notions of righteousness/virtue/gravitas); "dharmas" (plural) refer to the basic elements of consciousness or whatever ties experienced reality together

- Siddha: a man who had gained control over himself to the extent that he was in complete harmony with the cosmos, unaffected by external constraints

Reflection Questions

1. What are the differences between Theravada Buddhism and Mahayana Buddhism? What might be some of the effects of these differences on the life of an individual in each type of Buddhist society?

2. What does Buddhism teach is the cause of suffering? How can it be eliminated?

3. Compare and contrast Buddhist and Hindu ideas of rebirth and of god/gods.

Discussion Question

1. Summarize and explain what Buddhists believe, including the concept of enlightenment and nirvana. Compare and contrast these beliefs to that of Christianity.

Quiz

1. (T/F) The beginning of the Buddhist era marked a relative high point from which everything gradually degenerated.

2. (T/F) The historical facts regarding the first history of Buddhism in India are plentiful and highly regarded.

3. (T/F) The ultimate goal in Buddhism is the death of community or "the extinction of the whole."

4. (T/F) The first 500-year period of Buddhism focused on the rules of the Sangha.

5. (T/F) The second 500-year period began around the beginning of the Christian era when what became known as the Mahayana or "great vehicle" was formed.

6. During the third 500-year period of Buddhism, a man who had gained control over himself to the extent that he was in complete harmony with the cosmos and unaffected by external constraints was known as

   a) Tantra
   b) Siddha
   c) Monastic
   d) None of the above

7. The fourth 500-year period begins around 10.0 AD and features death and decline in

   a) Bangladesh
   b) Burma
   c) India
   d) Asia

8. During this time, invasions by _____ destroyed Buddhist centers of learning and civilization.

   a) British colonialists
   b) Other Hindu sects
   c) Pakistan
   d) Muslims

9. During the fifth 500-year period of Buddhism, the _____ school of Buddhism developed in China and was transported to Japan where it became popularized as Zen Buddhism.

   a) Burmese
   b) Zao
   c) Hinayana
   d) Chan

10. Buddhism has a vast number of scriptures usually divided into two groups: Dharma/Sutra (doctrinal texts) and

    a) Vinaya
    b) Pali
    c) Tripitaka
    d) Kathina

ANSWER KEY

1. T, 2. F, 3. F, 4. T, 5. T, 6. B, 7. C, 8. D, 9. D, 10. A

CHAPTER 13

The Moral Quest of Edward Conze

You Should Know

- Conze was one of the great Buddhist scholars of the twentieth century during which he helped shaped the reception of Buddhism in the English-speaking world.

- To understand Conze's scholarship requires placing it in the context of his passionate concern with the moral questions raised by war. He was a committed pacifist who was horrified at the brutality of modern warfare.

- This session presents the life of Conze in terms of what James Richardson identifies as "a conversion career," and then as the life of a mature Buddhist apologist.

- The life of Edward Conze is meant to throw new light on the development of Western Buddhism, its interaction with Christianity, and the important role played by Fascism and Marxism in shaping many twentieth-century Western Buddhists.

- In England Conze came to see himself as bogged down in a hopeless mire. What rescued him was his rediscovery of Buddhism. While recommitting himself to Buddhism, Conze discovered astrology and developed a love for it which remained with him for the rest of his life.

- The key to Conze's spiritual development appears to lie in the disillusionment he felt as a child with his parents' generation, the society in which he lived, and the actions of supposedly Christian leaders.

- Despite his outspoken opinions on the supernatural nature of religion, his scholarship was so good by the standards of his age that it was hard to reject his work. Therefore, although he never held a permanent academic position, his work laid the foundation for the development of Buddhist studies in the West.

- *The Memoirs of a Modern Gnostic*: written by Edward Conze to explore Buddhist ideas and philosophy, which carries an overriding theme as a passionate concern with the moral questions raised by war

Reflection Questions

1. Why, did Conze say, did he not want to visit a Buddhist land? Describe some of the events in Conze's life, and in the world during his lifetime, which led him to become, in his words, "disillusioned with the world as it is."

2. In what ways was Conze a 'Buddhist fundamentalist'?

3. Does Conze's life story make you curious about the backgrounds and shaping influences of other scholars and authors whose work you have read? Why or why not?

Discussion Question

1. Hexam describes Conze as "he was teasing Christian readers" and one particular remark was "typical of his ongoing interaction with Christianity and curious fascination with the Christian faith." In what way was Conze's Buddhism a reaction to Christianity? How did the two interact in Conze's life?

Quiz

1. (T/F) To understand Edward Conze's scholarship requires placing it in the context of his passionate concern with the moral questions raised by famine.

2. (T/F) Growing up in the heyday of the German Empire and strongly influenced by family, school, and Wandervoegel (a Boy Scout–type group some consider the cradle of National Socialism), Conze embraced a rabid anti-Semitism and an ultrapatriotic Pan-Germanic militarism.

3. (T/F) Conze first encountered Marxism during his school years when he visited a "working class" home of a friend where he was shocked by the barrenness he saw.

4. (T/F) Conze became a full-fledged Marxist until fleeing to England and leaving the Communist Party in 1933.

5. (T/F) Withdrawing from society in Britain, Conze practiced meditation for a time and almost killed himself through alcoholism.

6. (T/F) Returning to Buddhism, from about 1938 Conze devoted his energies to the study of the Mahayana.

7. (T/F) The key to Conze's spiritual development appears to lie in his disillusionment with his parents' generation, the society in which he lived, and the actions of supposedly Christian leaders.

8. (T/F) Conze castigated modern expressions of Judaism.

9. (T/F) Conze considered Buddhism a full-blooded religion wherein the supernatural as discovered via such means as horoscopes and psychic events plays a significant role.

10. (T/F) Conze applauded many Western Buddhist leaders upon learning many of them had embraced Facism or National Socialism in the 1920s and 1930s.

ANSWER KEY

1. F, 2. T, 3. T, 4. T, 5. F, 6. T, 7. T, 8. F, 9. T, 10. F

CHAPTER 14

The Other Yogic-Type Traditions

You Should Know

- Apart from the major types of Buddhism and Hinduism, several other traditions fall within the general rubric of yogic religions.

- Though few in number, Jains and Parsees merit mention; Sikhs are one of the largest small religions originating in the sphere of yogic tradition, albeit highly exclusive and essentially ethnic in nature.

- Mention should also be made of the once great Confucian and Taoist traditions which were virtually wiped out during the twentieth century; although these still have an ethical and social influence, they no longer exist as viable religious traditions on a worldwide scale.

- Jainism: one of the ancient Indian religions to emerge, centuries after the collapse of the Indus Valley civilization, out of the general social and religious matrix that created the complex Hindu tradition

- Nataputta Vardhamana: the founder of Jainism who is known as Mahavira, a title similar to "Christ" in Christianity

- Parsees: trace their origins to the prophet Zoroaster, who lived centuries before the Christian era and later fled to India as a result of Islamic persecution

- Confucianism: founded by the philosophical teacher Confucius whose work had religious overtones

- Sikhs: an Indian-based ethnic religious community with a rich tradition that is essentially uninterested in making converts

Reflection Questions

1. How did the two schools of Confucianism, associated respectively with Meng Tzu and Hsun Tzu, differ in their views of mankind? On what did they agree, and what common solutions did they propose?

2. Hexham describes ways in which Confucian and Taoist principles and practices still permeate Asian society, even as these systems of thought are no longer cohesively understood or put into practice. What traces of religious traditions and values do you see in your own society, even among those who do not profess any faith?

3. List five questions you would like to ask a Sikh man or woman about his or her belief and practice.

Discussion Question

1. Briefly summarize and explain the beliefs of the other Yogic-type traditions.

Quiz

1. _____ are one of the largest small religions originating in the sphere of yogic tradition.
   a) Sunni
   b) Shia
   c) Sikhs
   d) Sanskrits

2. _____ is one of the ancient Indian religions that emerged, centuries after the collapse of the Indus Valley civilization, out of the general social and religious matrix that created the complex Hindu tradition.
   a) Jainism
   b) Hinduism
   c) Buddhism
   d) Taoism

3. The traditional founder of the Jain tradition was an Indian sage Nataputta Vardhamana or "Mahavira," a title similar to "_____."

   a) Prophet
   b) Priest
   c) King
   d) Christ

4. The Jain scriptures are called _____.

   a) Puvaras
   b) Purim
   c) Parsees
   d) Paraclete

5. The _____ trace their origins to the prophet Zoroaster.

   a) Puvaras
   b) Purim
   c) Parsees
   d) Paraclete

6. The once great Confucian and _____ traditions were virtually wiped out during the twentieth century.

   a) Vardhamana
   b) Taoist
   c) Khalsa
   d) Avesta

7. _____'s first vision is believed to have involved an angel leading him into the presence of God or Ahura Mazda.

   a) Confucius
   b) Mencius
   c) Zoroaster
   d) Hsun Tzu

8. The founder of Taoism was

   a) Mao Zedung
   b) Kabir
   c) Hsun Tzu
   d) Lao Tzu

9. _____ is considered the founder of Sikhism and was conversant with both the Hindu and Muslim scriptures.

   a) Guru Nanak
   b) Adi Granth
   c) Granth Sahib
   d) Meng Tzu

10. Sikhs believe in one God, Sat Nam, which means _____ _____ in English.

    a) Holy One
    b) Sovereign God
    c) Truthful Name
    d) Just Ruler

ANSWER KEY

1. C, 2. A, 3. D, 4. A, 5. C, 6. B, 7. C, 8. D, 9. A, 10. C

CHAPTER 15

Early Judaism

You Should Know

Key Terms

- Talmud; Torah; Pentateuch; Apocrypha; Masoretic text; Septuagint; Hanukkah; Midrash; Jerusalem Talmud; Babylonian Talmud; Rabbinic Judaism

Key People and Locations

- Alexander the Great; Antiochus Epiphanes; Maccabees; Pompey; Herod the Great; Pontius Pilate; Florus

Key Points

- The ancient religion of Israel is not the same as Judaism which developed after the destruction of the Jerusalem temple in AD 70.

- Talking about Judaism is problematic because many Jews dispute the term almost as much as they dispute what it means to be Jewish. Jews belong to an identifiable ethnic group that is neither a religion nor a race; it is thus possible to have nonreligious Jews who practice Jewish rituals merely as a means of affirming their identity.

- Historically, Jews originated with the family of Abraham, but over time they incorporated people from many different families — what we now call nations and races — making any definition of Jewishness exceptionally difficult.

- Michael Fishbane states: "Judaism is thus the religious expression of the Jewish people from antiquity to the present day as it has tried to form and live a life of holiness before God."[1] This is the definition of Judaism in mind in this discussion.

- For Christians, Christianity is the fulfillment of the teachings of the Hebrew Bible and the natural completion of Judaism. For Jews, Christianity is a systematic distortion of Jewish religion that creates something almost totally unrecognizable.

- Talmud: vast collection of interpretations of the Jewish Scripture

- Torah: God's instrument for the creation of a covenantal people and is the true heritage of his people, a guide to life, the scrolls of the five books of Moses and teachings of those books understood within the context of the other Jewish scriptures and Jewish tradition

- Pentateuch: five books of Moses

- Apocryphy: supplemental books to the Hebrew Bible, including Tobit, Judith, Maccabees 1–4, Ezra, Ecclesiasticus, and the Wisdom of Solomon

Reflection Questions

1. How does the Jewish understanding of Torah differ from the Christian understanding of "the Law," or Pentateuch? What role does Torah play in Jewish theology?

2. Describe the relationship and chronology of the Torah, Midrash, and Talmud.

3. What event occasioned the transition from what Hexham calls the "Hebrew religion" to Judaism? What are some of the differences between the two?

Discussion Question

1. Briefly summarize and explain the history of Judaism.

---

1 Michael Fishbane, *Judaism* (San Francisco: Harper, 1987), 12

Quiz

1. (T/F) For Christians, Christianity is the fulfillment of the teachings of the Hebrew Bible and the natural completion of Judaism.

2. (T/F) For Jews, Christianity is a systematic distortion of Jewish religion that creates something almost totally unrecognizable.

3. (T/F) Hexham suggests it is not important to see Judaism as a religion in its own right, or to see it as totally separate from the Christian tradition. It is entirely legitimate to interpret it through a Christian lens.

4. (T/F) To understand how Jews view creation, we must look not to the Bible alone but to that vast collection of interpretation known as the Torah.

5. Jews read the biblical narratives differently than Christians. The story of Abraham can be seen as the founding story of Jewish origins, yet the most important event for Jews is the revelation of the _____ or giving of the law to Moses (Exodus 19).

   a) Torah
   b) Tanak
   c) Bible
   d) Apocrypha

6. The Hebrew Bible consists of the Pentateuch, the Prophets, and the Scriptures, but also includes a number of books called the _____.

   a) Torah
   b) Tanak
   c) Septuagint
   d) Apocrypha

7. Jewish scholars translated the Hebrew Bible into Greek in what is known as the _____.

   a) Torah
   b) Tanak
   c) Septuagint
   d) Apocrypha

8. The Jewish understanding of history is chronicled in the Old Testament of the Bible essentially up until the time of the return from _____ when the Jews were permitted to return to Judah and rebuild Jerusalem.

   a) Egyptian captivity
   b) Assyrian captivity
   c) Persian captivity
   d) Babylonian captivity

9. Judea was annexed by the kingdom of Syria and its Seleucid rulers who were Greek. One of their kings, _____, determined to unify his empire under one religion and sought to suppress Jewish worship and transform the Jerusalem temple to a Greek one.

   a) Antiochus Epiphanes
   b) Herod the Great
   c) Ramses
   d) Alexander the Great

10. In 166 BC a rebellion broke out under the priestly Maccabee family resulting in the independence of Judah, an event Jews today remember in the festival of _____.

    a) Passover
    b) Purim
    c) Hanukkah
    d) Ramadan

ANSWER KEY

1. T, 2. T, 3. F, 4. F, 5. A, 6. D, 7. C, 8. D, 9. A, 10. C

CHAPTER 16

Rabbinic and Other Judaism

You Should Know

- Jewish communities were established in northern Europe during the Roman Empire, particularly along the banks of the Danube and Rhine rivers. Cities like Mainz and Worms in German-speaking lands and Troyes and Sens in France became important Jewish centers that produced distinguished scholars. As tensions rose between Christianity and Islam leading to the eleventh-century Crusades, life for Jews became precarious and tragic.

- Around the seventh century AD, European Judaism had two major manifestations: Sephardic Jews of Spain, and Ashkenazi Jews of northern Europe. It is important to remember that Judaism defined itself not as a creed along the lines of Christianity and Islam, but as a way of life.

- At the core of traditional or rabbinic Judaism was "the matrix of traditional Jewish life" (Fishbane) kept alive by liturgical practices, communal involvement, and the daily life of Jewish families.

- Often living in hostile and dangerous environments, Jews in both the Christian and Muslim worlds looked inward to their own people for solace and protection. These traumatic times created memories of "tears and martyrdom." In Muslim lands both Jews and Christians shared the status of *dhimmitude* (second-class citizens), protected by law but not as well as true Muslims to whom they were subservient. In Christian lands Jews were protected by secular rulers and church authorities against the whim of the populace. In both areas, the situation of Jews was precarious at best.

- Most importantly, Jewish isolation from surrounding society brought about the acceptance of "love and care for fellow Jews" as a central value of Judaism; based on the belief that "all Jews are responsible one for another," this principle has been key in uniting Jews over the centuries.

- Sephardic Judaism identified Jews living in the Iberian Peninsula until expelled by Spain in 1492. The majority took refuge in Muslim lands moving to Constantinople, Egypt, and North Africa; others settled in Portugal and northern Europe, particularly the Netherlands.

- Ashkenazy Judaism originated in northern Europe particularly in German-speaking lands in the tenth century. Ashkenazi Jews later spread to the Netherlands, Poland, Russia, and eastern Europe. In Europe they distinguished themselves with high levels of literacy and education; many became moneylenders, doctors, and lawyers.

- The main difference between the Sephardic and Ashkenazi forms of Judaism is found in the liturgy and in cultural practices within families. Liturgically, the order and number of prayers, the type of script used to write Torah scrolls, the storage and handling of the scrolls, the use of lights, and various other details differed. Sephardic Jews refuse to eat fish and milk in the same meal whereas Ashkenazi Jews will. Approximately 17 percent of Jews are non-Ashkenazi, the majority of these being Sephardic. Within Israel, Sephardic Jews number around 50 percent, making Israeli Jews significantly different than others in this respect.

Reflection Questions

1. Describe at least three pre-eighteenth-century instances, in three different locations, in which the Jews' minority status in European societies made them easy targets for suspicion and blame. Describe at least three events which Hexham highlights as having laid the foundation for later anti-Semitism.

2. How did each of these nineteenth-century movements within Judaism seek to adapt Jewish culture and practice to their contemporary surroundings and ways of life: Reform Judaism, Conservative Judaism, and Hirsch's neo-Orthodoxy?

3. How was Zionism impacted by the Holocaust and, later, by the Six-Day War of 1967? Does your faith community have a particular stance or set of beliefs about the Jews, or about the political entity of Israel and its future? Explain those beliefs, and why you agree or disagree with them.

Discussion Question

1. Briefly summarize and explain Rabbini and other forms of Judaism explored in this session.

Quiz

1. Jewish communities were established in northern Europe during the Roman Empire particularly along the banks of the Danube and Rhine Rivers; cities like _____ and _____ in German-speaking lands became important Jewish centers.

   a) Stuttgart and Berlin
   b) Mainz and Worms
   c) Bonn and Hamburg
   d) All of the above

2. Around the seventh century AD, European Judaism had two major manifestations, one of which was called Sephardic Jews who lived in

   a) Spain
   b) France
   c) Germany
   d) The Netherlands

3. The other manifestation of Jews were known as the _____ Jews of northern Europe.

   a) Orthodox
   b) Ashkenazi
   c) Messianic
   d) Hasidic

4. In Muslim lands both Jews and Christians shared the status of

   a) Dhimmitude
   b) Second-class citizens
   c) Holocaust survivors
   d) A & B

5. Differences between the Sephardic and Ashkenazi forms of Judaism are found in

   a) The order and number of prayers and the type of script used to write Torah scrolls
   b) The liturgy and the cultural practices within families
   c) Certain foods they do or do not eat
   d) All of the above

6. During the _____, proclaimed by Pope Urban II to defend Christian pilgrims visiting the Holy Land, military leaders effected the massacre of scores of Jews.

   a) Millennium War
   b) First Crusade
   c) Second Crusade
   d) Twenty-Seven-Day War

7. During the Third Crusade, this bloodlust spread to _____ where a Jewish community in one of its cities was massacred.

   a) Ireland
   b) The Netherlands
   c) Germany
   d) England

8. The great Jewish philosopher _____ had to flee Muslim oppression numerous times.

a) Cicero
   b) Maimonides
   c) Benado
   d) Jacobus

9. From the early Middle Ages, Jews migrated through Germany and areas of the Byzantine Empire into
   a) Prussia and the Rhineland
   b) Prussia and Russia
   c) Russia and Poland
   d) All of the above

10. The extending of rights to Jews in the fourteenth century by King Casimir II and the Grand Duke of Lithuania had a dark side which affected the fate of Jews in modern times. Being an educated people, the Jews became good recruits for government service with many becoming tax collectors, estate managers, and government agents and were feared by the common people who saw them as oppressors. These developments laid a foundation for
   a) The Thirty Years' War
   b) Anti-Semitism
   c) The Protestant Reformation
   d) The Industrial Revolution

ANSWER KEY

1. B, 2. A, 3. B, 4. D, 5. D, 6. B, 7. D, 8. B, 9. C, 10. B

CHAPTER 17

Jewish Faith and Practice

You Should Know

- Moses Maimonides: the most famous of all Jewish philosophers who was one of the great medieval exponents of Aristotle. He sought to preserve Torah and defend it against all criticism, and to provide Jews with a creed, which he wrote in poetic form.

- Rosh Hashana: the first day of Tishrei (Jewish new year) marks the creation of the world and the opening of the book of life by God. It is a communal celebration in the synagogue.

- Yom Kippur (Day of Atonement): the holiest, most solemn day in the Jewish year, when Jews come to terms with themselves and make peace with any they have wronged

- Hanukkah: celebration in rememberance of the miracle that took place when a sacred lamp burned for eight days after the Jewish revolt against Syrian domination. It is a merry time of joy, blessing, and the exchange of gifts commemorated by lighting of the menorah, an eight-branch candlestick.

- Pesach (the Feast of Passover): recalls the liberation of Israel from Egyptian bondage. Unleavened bread or *matzot* is eaten as is a special meal called the *seder*.

- Purim: joyful feast on the fourteenth of Adar celebrating the Old Testament story of Esther and the preservation of the Jews

- Shavuot: a harvest festival celebrating the reception of the Ten Commandments by Moses

- Bahir: the first kabbalistic text produced by a group of Jewish mystics that flourished in France in the twelfth century

Reflection Questions

1. What similarities do you find between German-based Jewish mysticism and Buddhist philosophy? What differences do you recognize?

2. Explain two fundamental differences between the law of Moses and Hammurabi's Code.

3. How would you respond to Jacob Neusner's assertions that Jesus calls into question the primary Jewish duties/values of family and Sabbath, and therefore a Jew cannot accept Jesus's teachings?

Discussion Question

1. Briefly summarize and explain Jewish faith and practice, paying attention to Jewish philosophy and mysticism, as well as key Jewish ideas and piety.

Quiz

1. His *Guide for the Perplexed* is one of the great classics of medieval thought:
    a) Aristotle
    b) Moses Mendelssohn
    c) Moses Maimonides
    d) Martin Buber

2. This eighteenth century Jewish philosopher wrote the two-volume work *Concerning the Amelioration of the Civil Status of the Jews* (1781) and had a tremendous influence in helping to change public attitudes toward Jews.
    a) Martin Buber
    b) Moses Maimonides

c) Moses Mendelssohn
d) Eleazer Segal

3. Although Jewish mystical systems clearly existed around Christ's time, it was not until the _____ that any clear idea emerged regarding such.

   a) European Middle Ages
   b) Destruction of the Temple in 70 AD
   c) Thirty Years' War
   d) First Crusade

4. The three main centers of Jewish mysticism during the period referred to in number 3 were Germany, Spain, and _____.

   a) Italy
   b) France
   c) Southern France
   d) Austria

5. (T/F) The communities of mystics mentioned in number 4 would develop the concept of a pious individual named David as a role model.

6. (T/F) A group of Jewish mystics that flourished in France in the twelfth century produced the first kabbalistic text known as the *Bahir*.

7. (T/F) Although Jewish communities were demoralized at this time (when one leader converted to Islam and Jews in Poland were harassed and massacred), the Hasidic movement arose with a message of personal piety and salvation.

8. _____ was founded by a Pole, Israel ben Eliezer.

   a) Judaism
   b) Kabbalism
   c) Hasidism
   d) Sunnism

9. The reality of an _____ has been disputed in Judaism, although today most Jews affirm such.

   a) Salvation
   b) Afterlife

c) Creation
d) Sin

10. Jews believe creation took place _____ years before Christ's birth. Thus, to know which Jewish year it is, add this figure to whatever date it is today.

   a) 3760
   b) 4123
   c) 2 million
   d) 8 billion

ANSWER KEY
1. C, 2. C, 3. A, 4. C, 5. F, 6. T, 7. T, 8. C, 9. B, 10. A

CHAPTER 18

Martin Buber's Zionist Spirituality

You Should Know

- Arguably, more than any other modern Jewish thinker, Martin Buber has profoundly influenced Christian theology; he has also had an enormous effect on Jewish thinking and practice through his philosophical works and studies of Hasidism.

- For Buber the Hebrew Bible was a record of Israel's experience with God and therefore central to his faith. He was not a Bible-believer like most evangelical Christians; in Buber's view Scripture expresses the longings of men and women for God but does not present a correct understanding of God. Buber hoped that by rejecting a literal view of the Bible in favor of rational ethics and a living religious experience, the essence of Judaism would be preserved. When choosing between God and Scripture, a good Jew chooses God.

- Ludwig Feuerbach (1804–1872) was the most influential writer for Buber because "unlike Kant," Feuerbach "wishes to make the whole person, not human cognition, the beginning of philosophizing."[2] By "man," Buber understood Feuerbach to not mean man as individual but man with man — a connection of I and Thou, an idea which became the title for his most famous book, *I and Thou*.

- Buber explained his understanding of God via his encounter with Reverend Hechler, a pro-Zionist Christian pastor with a firm belief in biblical prophecy. His question of Buber: "Do you believe

---

2 Martin Buber, *Between Man and Man*, trans. Ronald Gregor Smith (London: Routledge and Kegan Paul, 1947), 146.

in God?" struck Buber to his core; he responded: "If to believe in [God] means to be able to talk to him, then I believe in God."[3]

- Buber's philosophy was rooted in Ludwig Feuerbach's insight into the primary importance of relations; thus Buber said: "the primary word I-Thou establishes a world of relation,"[4] — meaning, one discovers personhood by entering into relationship with others. Reality is to be found only in what Buber calls "the real twofold entity I and Thou."[5] Therefore, all reality is shared reality.

- Buber's work falls into the category of a Jewish response to the problem of revelation and taps the roots of the Jewish tradition. Buber's revelation is a revelation of a people, not a revealed scripture even though the Torah (a scripture) binds the people together.

- In contrast to Buber's spirituality, Christian revelation rests on the authority of revelation itself, not upon a particular people bound together by genetic inheritance. For Buber, to talk of good news from God mediated through Jesus involves preoccupation with experience, and experience of or with Jesus can never be pure revelation.

- Buber saw Zionism as a dynamic way of life and not simply a political creed. For him the appeal lay in its ability to revitalize the Jewish people and revive eternal Israel through a combination of modern philosophical reasoning, mystical experience, and messianic expectations. From the time he embraced Zionism until his death, he never doubted that this was the only solution for the survival of Judaism.

Reflection Questions

1. To Buber, what was "the uniqueness of Israel," and how could the Jewish people persist?

---

[3] Martin Buber, *Meetings: Autobiographical Fragments* (London: Routledge, 2002; first published 1967), 62.

[4] Martin Buber, *I and Thou* (Edinburgh: T&T Clark, 1958), 3.

[5] Ibid., 59.

2. How does Buber's vision of the mission of the Jewish people compare with your understanding of the mission of the Christian church?

3. Does Buber claim that the Bible is God's revelation of himself to humanity? How would you explain Buber's use of the Bible and of the term "revelation"?

Discussion Question

1. Summarize and explain Martin Buber's Zionist spirituality.

Quiz

1. Arguably, more than any other modern Jewish thinker, Martin Buber has profoundly influenced _____.

   a) Jewish theology
   b) Christian theology
   c) Buddhist theology
   d) Muslim theology

2. The title of Buber's most famous book was _____.

   a) *You and Me*
   b) *Thou and I*
   c) *I and Thou*
   d) *Me and You*

3. Buber's work falls into the category of a Jewish response to the problem of _____.

   a) Revelation
   b) Salvation
   c) Eternity
   d) Being

4. In reading the works of _____ Buber was captivated by the Zionist vision.

   a) Friedrich Nietzsche
   b) John Calvin

c) Martin Luther
   d) Theodor Herzl

5. Buber always viewed Zionism as a dynamic way of life and not simply a _____.

   a) Political creed
   b) Theological creed
   c) Spiritual creed
   d) Religious creed

6. Zionism for Buber was not some narrow and exclusive preserve of Jews but an ideal capable of _____.

   a) Engaging the world
   b) Condemning the world
   c) Embracing the world
   d) Experiencing the world

7. Buber's Zionism became the key to his thought and freed him from the challenging yet ultimately oppressive philosophy of the German thinker _____.

   a) Friedrich Nietzsche
   b) John Calvin
   c) Martin Luther
   d) Theodor Herzl

8. As a German Jew, Buber lived in a peculiar tension arising from his Jewish heritage and the lure of _____ which, like many intellectuals, he loved.

   a) German spirituality
   b) German politics
   c) German religion
   d) German culture

9. In his address, _____ (1934), Buber articulated his more mature views on Zionism, arguing that the Jews "were hurled into the abyss of the world" by the Roman destruction of Jerusalem.

   a) "The German in the World"
   b) "The Christian in the World"

c) "The Jew in the World"
d) "The Zionist in the World"

10. (T/F) Long before Nazism, Buber advocated that Jews must migrate to Palestine. But it was not the destiny of Jews merely to occupy the land. Rather, Jews could grow and prosper only if they ensured that peoples around them shared their joy and prosperity.

ANSWER KEY

1. B, 2. C, 3. A, 4. D, 5. A, 6. C, 7. A, 8. D, 9. C, 10. T

CHAPTER 19

Christianity

You Should Know

- Unlike other major religions, Christians have no difficulty using the name of Christ, who they see as the founder of their religion, as part of their faith's name. This is one of the peculiarities of Christianity.

- Even writers such as the famous American polemicist Thomas Paine (1737–1809), who frequently attacked Christianity and the church, retained great respect for Jesus. It should thus be noted that whereas Jesus is regarded with such respect, other leaders including Abraham, Moses, and Muhammad, are not venerated in this way by anyone other than their followers in Judaism and Islam. The centrality of Jesus to both the Christian message and the world history merits special consideration.

- Most college and university courses approach Christianity in a different manner than they do other religious traditions. Instead of presenting Christianity as it is practiced in numerous Christian communities, they tend to concentrate on textual studies and critical issues about the reliability of the Bible; thus Christianity is often presented in an essentially negative manner while other religions are presented in a comparatively positive way.

- An attempt is made here to deal with Christianity in the way that other religions are shown in introductory courses; that is, as a holistic religious tradition in which the experience of believers is given precedence. Accordingly, and in the tradition of intellectual history, Christianity is viewed historically, not from a theological perspective.

- Our sources of information about Jesus come primarily from the New Testament, which provides a complex portrayal of this important religious leader.

- Christians have held that Matthew's gospel was the first gospel and was written for Jews, that Mark's gospel was a condensed account of the life of Jesus written for Romans, and that Luke's gospel was written primarily with Greeks in mind. Then they explained that John's gospel was written last, to bring out in a more detailed way the spiritual significance of the stories told in the other three gospels.

- Various deistic writers, of whom Thomas Paine is probably the best example, denied that gospels were eyewitness accounts, and some, like Paine, suggested that they were written hundreds of years after the event.

- On the basis of what the New Testament teaches about Jesus, Christians believe that he was the incarnation of God. Yet they do not believe that he was a demigod like the Greek gods, many of whom were born through the union of gods with humans to produce a creature that is half god and half human. Rather, Christians argue that the New Testament teaches that Jesus is fully God and fully human.

- "Q" document: a hypothetical common source of material used in the Synoptic Gospels

Reflection Questions

1. What does Auerbach mean when he says that the Bible's claim to truth is "tyrannical"? What about the Bible's literary style does he say sets it apart from classical epics? Describe how you see this style used in a particular biblical passage.

2. In light of the new "science" of biblical criticism developed throughout the nineteenth century, the traditional view derived from the arguments of the church fathers that Matthew's is the earliest

gospel was rejected, and it was argued that Mark's gospel must be the earliest. Explain.

3. Describe the Christian view of the Hebrew Bible. How might a Christian describe the Hebrew Bible's relationship to the New Testament? How might a Jew describe that same relationship?

Discussion Question

1. Explain in your own words how the key events of Christianity — Jesus's death and resurrection — might connect with the Christian doctrine of the fall of man.

Quiz

1. (T/F) As compared to other religious figures, the centrality of Jesus to both the Christian message and world history merits special consideration.

2. (T/F) Hexham maintains that most college/university courses approach Christianity in a different manner than they do other religious traditions. Instead of presenting Christianity as it is practiced in numerous Christian communities, they tend to concentrate on textual studies and critical issues about the reliability of the Bible. Christianity is thus often presented in an essentially negative manner while other religions are presented in a comparatively positive way.

3. (T/F) Johann Gottfried von Herder is primarily remembered as among those who suggested the Gospels were actually written hundreds of years after the events they identify.

4. (T/F) As the new "science" of biblical criticism arose in the nineteenth century, scholars claimed to have identified various sources in the text of the New Testament. The most famous of these is the so-called "Q" document, which is said to lie behind the Synoptic Gospels.

5. The _____ is the best attested of all ancient manuscripts.

   a) Torah
   b) The Old Testament
   c) The New Testament
   d) Didache

6. Joseph Ratzinger, who has also held the office of _____, argues in his book *Jesus of Nazareth* that from the beginning of his ministry, Christ's intent was to found the Christian church.

   a) Elder
   b) Deacon
   c) Priest
   d) Pope

7. A certain theology teaches that Jesus went further than simply founding a church and appointed one of his disciples, Peter, to be its head. Other Christians dispute that the _____ was directly founded by Jesus in this way.

   a) Roman Catholic Church
   b) Church of England
   c) Russian Orthodox Church
   d) Ukranian Orthodox Church

8. According to Christians, God created the universe out of _____ then proceeded to form the earth and populate it with plants, animals, and the first humans (Adam and Eve).

   a) Dust
   b) Nothing
   c) Ex nihilo
   d) B & C

9. Without a grasp of the _____, it is not possible to truly understand the meaning of Christianity.

   a) Jewish scriptures
   b) Exodus
   c) Eschaton
   d) New Testament

10. For Christians, the story of the _____ is a type/analogy of redemption.
   a) Jewish scriptures
   b) Exodus
   c) Eschaton
   d) New Testament

ANSWER KEY
1. T, 2. T, 3. F, 4. F, 5. C, 6. D, 7. A, 8. D, 9. A, 10. B

CHAPTER 20

Christian History

You Should Know

Key People and Locations

- Constantine; Theodosius; Venerable Bede; Jesuits; Martin Luther; John Calvin; Ignatius Loyola; Philipp Jakob Spener; Johann Arndt; August Hermann Francke; Karl Barth; Dietrich Bonhoeffer; Billy Graham; Pope John Paul II; Pope Benedict XVI

Noteworthy Backgrounds

- From the time of the early church until the destruction of the Western Roman Empire in the fifth century, Christian churches were established in the Roman Empire and beyond. Maps from this time are misleading since they create the impression that the civilized world consisted only of the Roman Empire, India, and China; but other civilizations did exist including a thriving Persian Empire, Armenia, and various parts of Africa.

- When thinking about the expansion of the Christian church, therefore, we must realize that it very quickly established itself beyond the borders of the Roman Empire in both friendly regions of Africa and hostile regions of the Persian Empire. As well, there is growing evidence that Christian missionaries reached India and China by the second century.

- Nevertheless, this account of Christian history will primarily focus on Western Europe because it was in these areas that the forms of Christianity which dominate the world today came to fruition.

- Edict of Milan: an edict of tolerance to stop the official persecution of Christians issued by Emperor Constantine

- Council of Nicea: the most important church council held in AD 325 in which the doctrine of the person of Jesus Christ and his relationship to God was carefully worked out in what became known as the doctrine of the incarnation, which teaches that God became man

- Protestant Reformation: usually said to have begun on 31 October 1517, when Luther nailed ninety-five theses onto the door of the palace church in Wittenberg as a way to reform the church and remove practices like indulgences, which he believed were contrary to the clear teaching of Scripture

- Counter-Reformation: a remarkable renewal movement launched by the Roman Catholic Church spearheaded by the Jesuits, founded in 1540 by Ignatius Loyola

- Martin Luther: a German monk largely responsible for launching the Protestant Reformation when he issued his ninety-five theses questioning the basis of salvation as taught by the Catholic Church, in particular the practice of selling indulgences, which were said to free people from their sins

- Pope John Paul II: a popular Polish pope who took a stand against the cultural relativism of accommodation to the times

Reflection Questions

1. The earliest disciples of Jesus were all Jews, and yet in Christianity, unlike in Judaism, orthodoxy (right belief) took primacy over orthopraxy (right practice). Propose at least two suggestions as to why this shift took place.

2. Of pre-tenth-century Europe, Hexham writes, "This was a world very unlike our own . . ." What similarities do you see between his description of the miraculous in this setting and his explanation of power and primal experiences in Chapters 3 and 4 ("African Religious Traditions" and "Witchcraft and Sorcery")? What explanation does your own worldview supply for the miracles and spiritual battles recorded by early European Christians?

3. What was Martin Luther's original intent in questioning doctrines and practices of the Catholic Church? In three sentences, summarize the chain of cause and effect from Luther's first protest to the Thirty Years' War, one hundred years later.

Discussion Question

1. Briefly summarize and explain the spread of global Christianity from Judea out into the rest of the world over the course of history.

Quiz

1. Posted Ninety-Five Theses to the church door in Wittenberg launching the Reformation.

    a) Martin Luther
    b) Philipp Jakob Spener
    c) Augustine of Hippo
    d) John Calvin

2. Established the doctrine of the incarnation: Jesus was fully God and fully man.

    a) Council of Nicea
    b) Peace of Westphalia
    c) Edict of Milan
    d) Council of Chalcedon

3. An influential Lutheran pietist preacher in the seventeenth century.

    a) Martin Luther
    b) Philipp Jakob Spener
    c) Augustine of Hippo
    d) Christian Wolff

4. Roman emperor who made Christianity the official religion of the empire.

a) Emperor Constantine
b) Emperor Bede
c) Emperor Loyola
d) Emperor Theodosius

5. Early Christian theologian who wrote *The City of God*.

a) Philipp Jakob Spener
b) Augustine of Hippo
c) John Calvin
d) Venerable Bede

6. German rationalist whose thinking promoted a disdain for Christian orthodoxy.

a) Martin Luther
b) Philipp Jakob Spener
c) Christian Wolff
d) John Calvin

7. Marked the end of the Thirty Years' War in 1648.

a) Council of Nicea
b) Edict of Milan
c) Peace of Westphalia
d) 95 Theses

8. Argued that Scripture allowed for only believing adults to be baptized.

a) Baptists
b) Catholics
c) Anglicans
d) Calvinists

9. A declaration of toleration of Christianity and cessation of persecution.

a) Council of Nicea
b) Edict of Milan
c) Peace of Westphalia
d) 95 Theses

10. He wrote *The Ecclesiastical History of English People* in 731.
    a) John Calvin
    b) Venerable Bede
    c) Ignatius Loyola
    d) Augustine

ANSWER KEY

1. A, 2. A, 3. B, 4. D, 5. B, 6. C, 7. C, 8. A, 9. B, 10. B

CHAPTER 21

Christian Faith and Practice

You Should Know

- The doctrines of creation, fall, and redemption form the core of Christian belief and define the relationship between God and mankind. After the creation of a perfect world, mistrust entered the relationship between humanity and God with the fall. To redeem humans from suspicion and regression, God engaged in an act of infinite love—providing Jesus to restore the broken trust.

- Unlike other major world religions, Christianity strongly emphasizes correct belief. It is *orthopraxis*, or the way people live, that is decisive in determining who is a Jew or a Muslim; similarly, in Buddhism and Hinduism, practice has traditionally been far more important than doctrines. Things are so different in this regard in Christianity that some criticize it as being an intellectual construct rather than a living practice.

- The Christian emphasis on belief, or what goes on inside a person, goes back to the teachings of Jesus where he consistently makes one's intent, not action, the fundamental issue in determining whether something is right or wrong. Following this example, the early disciples preached a message that demanded an intellectual decision.

- The New Testament epistles record creedlike statements, expressing the essence of the Christian faith in terms of the affirmation of explicit beliefs (Colossians 1:1–20); knowledge and acceptance of propositional truth is the key issue. Belief is not separated from practice since faith and works go together in that works grow out of faith.

- Postmillennialism: the more historical position, being held by the majority of Christians throughout history. It holds that the gospel must be preached to every nation, after which there will be a thousand years of peace before Christ returns to judge people and nations.

- Premillennialism: the dominant mode of eschatology in North America in the nineteenth century, believing that society will disintegrate into chaos before the second coming of Christ. Instead of a thousand years of peace, there will be universal unrest and widespread persecution of Christians.

- Dispensationalism: a variation of premillennialism that was popularized by the *Scofield Reference Bible* (1909) and is taught at such places as the influential Dallas Theological Seminary. Dispensationalism adopts the basic premillennial scheme but divides history into seven time periods, or dispensations, during which God is said to have dealt with humanity on the basis of different expectations.

- Charismatics: Christians who believe that *glossolalia*, or "speaking in tongues"; healing the sick; prophecy; and other "gifts of the Spirit" are signs of "the last days"

- Sacraments: a set of ceremonies to mark the passage of an individual's life; a religious rite in which God is believed to be uniquely active; "a visible sign of an invisible reality"

Reflection Questions

1. Describe the contrast between faith and legalism in the Christian tradition. How does the Christian definition of faith as Hexham explains it align with your own understanding of the concept, and with the ways you have heard it explained in Christian contexts?

2. How might a postmillennialist speak differently about contemporary events than a premillennialist? How might his or her eschatology affect his or her daily outlook?

3. How does Hexham describe the way in which different groups defend their positions about the Christian sacraments? What priorities do you see as shared between all groups in this discussion?

Discussion Question

1. Summarize and explain the doctrines of creation, fall, and redemption that form the core of Christian belief.

Quiz

1. Unlike other major world religions, Christianity strongly emphasizes
    a) Memorization of its scriptures
    b) Correct belief
    c) Celebration of its holy days
    d) All of the above

2. The Christian emphasis on what goes on inside a person goes back to the teachings of Jesus where he consistently makes one's _____, not action, the fundamental issue in determining whether something is right or wrong.
    a) Prayers
    b) Thoughts
    c) Intent
    d) Performance

3. All Christians believe that a living relationship with God is through _____, an act of trust based upon knowledge of God and his deeds. _____ is not a blind leap into the dark but a confident step into enlightenment regarding the nature and love of God.
    a) Intent
    b) Faith

c) Prayer

d) Hope

4. Inspiration for this Christian understanding (see number 3) is found in the Old Testament story of

   a) Abraham
   b) Sarah
   c) Isaac
   d) Ezekiel

5. (T/F) Ideas about the return of Christ give many contemporary Christians their distinctive emphasis.

6. (T/F) Postmillennialism is a nineteenth-century view popularized by John N. Darby (1800–1882) and the dominant mode of interpretation in North America. It teaches that society will deteriorate into chaos before Christ's return so that instead of a thousand years of peace, there will be universal unrest and persecution of Christians.

7. (T/F) Premillennialism is the historical view that asserts the gospel must be preached to every nation, after which a thousand years of peace will prevail before Christ returns as judge.

8. _____ is a variation of premillennialism popularized by the *Scofield Reference Bible* (1909).

   a) Fundamentalism
   b) Dispensationalism
   c) Evangelicalism
   d) Scofieldism

9. One of the important differences between the postmillennial and premillennial views is related to the biblical teaching about _____.

   a) The Church
   b) America
   c) Israel
   d) Palestine

10. Christians have significant disagreements regarding the meaning and means of both of the main _____.
   a) Doctrines
   b) Sacraments
   c) Practices
   d) Prayers

ANSWER KEY

1. B, 2. C, 3. B, 4. A, 5. T, 6. F, 7. F, 8. D, 9. C, 10. B

CHAPTER 22

Christian Politics according to Abraham Kuyper

You Should Know

- Born in 1837, upon earning a doctorate in theology Abraham Kuyper was ordained a minister in the Dutch Reformed Church wherein he converted from advanced theological liberalism to a living faith in Christ as Lord.

- Influenced by Willem Bilderdijk (1756–1831) and Guillaume Groen van Prinsterer (1801–1876), Kuyper helped found the first modern Dutch political party, the Anti-Revolutionary Party, and entered parliament to represent that new party. In 1880 he founded the Free University of Amsterdam and in 1886 led a secession movement from the Dutch Reformed Church to found his own independent Reformed Church.

- Like Calvin, Kuyper does not believe that any one form of government is in itself right for all times and places. Rather, the form that government takes is bound up with changes in historical and social circumstances. This position he traces back to Augustine.

- In 1891 Kuyper launched a series of attacks on capitalism, pleading for a form of Christian socialism. The Anti-Revolutionaries came to power in 1888 with a small majority. Following a split in ranks, in 1900 Kuyper's party gained undisputed power in parliament and he became prime minister in 1901 until his defeat at the polls in 1905. He retired from active politics in 1913 and died in 1920.

- Anyone wishing to understand modern North American Christianity needs to recognize that since the 1980s evangelical Christianity has undergone a remarkable political transformation. Until about 1970 the majority of evangelicals were convinced religion and politics did not mix and should not be mixed. Today, however, many believe that politics and Christianity cannot be separated, although more recent developments appear to be leading some American evangelicals to retreat from their involvement in politics.

- According to American Catholic sociologist Andrew Greeley, a small majority of the newly politicized evangelical and fundamentalist Christians are supporters of the New Christian Right, a large minority are political moderates, while a small minority such as Sojourners are on the radical left.

- What is noteworthy is that some leaders on both left and right trace their political thought and involvement to the work of Dutch theologian and statesman Abraham Kuyper (1837–1920). It is therefore helpful to know something of his life and thought to understand such.

- Three fundamental relationships: (1) our relation *to God*; (2) our relation *to man*; (3) our relation to *the world*.

- Three duties of the state to perform: (1) it must draw a boundary between the dif-ferent spheres to avoid social conflict; (2) it must defend individuals and weak elements within each sphere; (3) it must coerce all the separate spheres of society to support the state and uphold its legitimate functions.

Reflection Questions

1. Abraham Kuyper said all "such general systems of life" revolve around three fundamental relationships. What are those relationships, and how did he see Calvinism finding a right balance between them?

2. According to Kuyper, what are the three duties of the state toward the other spheres of human society? Does your own government fulfill

these three duties? Describe an example. Does your government go beyond these three duties to exercise further power within the spheres of society and church? Describe an example of how it does or does not.

3. Explain why, as Hexham puts it, Kuyper's theories have the potential to be a "truly Christian third way," not falling neatly into existing radical and conservative categories. Do the Christians you know seem to be seeking a "third way" of political engagement based on Scripture? Why or why not?

Discussion Question

1. Why, did Kuyper argue, was the idea of a unified state church unwise? Many European nations still have one officially established state church (denomination). List at least three nations with state churches today. How, in your opinion, do the teachings of the New Testament support, refute, or deny the idea of state religion?

Quiz

1. Hexham asserts that anyone wishing to understand modern North American Christianity needs to recognize that since the 1980s _____ Christianity has undergone a remarkable political transformation.

    a) Fundamentalist
    b) Protestant
    c) Catholic
    d) Evangelical

2. According to American Catholic sociologist Andrew Greeley a small majority of the newly politicized evangelical and fundamentalist Christians are supporters of the _____.

    a) New Christian Left
    b) New Christian Right
    c) Old Christian Right
    d) Old Christian Left

3. The earliest systematic expression of Abraham Kuyper's thought in English is found in his 1898 Stone Lectures, published as _____.
   a) Lectures on Calvinism
   b) Lectures on Lutheranism
   c) Lectures on Thomism
   d) Lectures on Augustine

4. Kuyper supported certain ideals called "anti-revolutionary principles" and helped found the _____.
   a) First modern German political party
   b) First modern English political party
   c) First modern Dutch political party
   d) First modern French political party

5. Kuyper taught that life revolves around three fundamental relationships with God, mankind, and the world. In _____ alone, he argued, one finds the right balance between these vital relationships.
   a) Evangelicalism
   b) Reformed theology
   c) Calvinism
   d) Modernism

6. The determinative principle for Calvinist political theory as argued by Kuyper in his writings and lectures is "the _____ of the Triune God over the whole Cosmos."
   a) Presence
   b) Reality
   c) Providence
   d) Sovereignty

7. Kuyper never defined what he means by "_____" yet appears to mean the civil government as recognized by the citizens of a country and by foreign powers.
   a) The authorities
   b) The state
   c) The government
   d) The establishment

8. (T/F) Kuyper rejected theocracy, teaching that the state has three duties to perform including: to draw a boundary between the different spheres, to avoid social conflict, and to coerce the separate spheres to support the state and uphold its legitimate functions.

9. (T/F) Kuyper believed that implicit in Calvin's teaching about liberty of the conscience is the ideal of a state church in a free society.

10. (T/F) In developing Calvinist themes Kuyper believed he was carrying on the task of reformation.

ANSWER KEY

1. D, 2. B, 3. A, 4. C, 5. C, 6. D, 7. B, 8. T, 9. F, 10. T

CHAPTER 23

The Challenge of Islam

You Should Know

- In the post-9/11 world, it is particularly important to understand the presuppositions and orientation behind any writer's attempts to interpret what Islam does and does not teach.

- This session attempts to understand Islam as it is presented by best-selling Muslim scholars in the Muslim world whose works are popular in English translation among committed Muslims living in the English-speaking world. It will be supplemented by academic studies written by Western-educated scholars, most of whom are non-Muslim; thus the understanding of Islam presented here is significantly different on some issues from that found in most other religious studies textbooks.

- The prominent, popular Egyptian Muslim writer, Sayyid Qutb (1906–1966) considered scholarly interpretations of Islam such as those found in popular religious texts to be "wily attacks of orientalists" who seek to destroy the faith by reinterpreting its core concepts in terms of secularizing Western ideas. Qutb is usually dismissed as an extremist by Western scholars of Islam, yet his works are immensely popular throughout the Muslim world and among Muslims living in Western countries.

- Our knowledge of Muhammad and his ways comes not from the Qur'an, which is a book of revelation, but from a body of literature known as the *Hadith*. His wife Aisha is said to have played a key role in compiling various sayings attributed to Muhammad after his death. This collection is believed to be the basis of the *Hadith* for Sunni Muslims. Since the Hadith is vast, other Muslim groups

- often use different collections and which Hadith are emphasized by any one group may vary.

- Sunni Islam believes that the Prophet Muhammad was guided by God in all his actions and words and was therefore able to see into the hearts of men and women and judge them according to their true nature. For them, the military victory of Abu Bakr's generals and of his Umayyad successors proves the wisdom and insight of the Prophet in accepting the full integration of the Quraysh tribe, particularly the Umayyad clan, into the Muslim community.

- At the core of Wahhabi Islam is a call to return to the pure teachings of the Qur'an and the example of the Prophet. It is the most important of reform movements that developed within the Sunni community, and is the official version of Islam in Saudi Arabia.

- The second largest Muslim community, the Shia, take a very different view of things. They are the followers of Ali, who remained loyal to Muhammad and his children, particularly those born to Muhammad's daughter Fatima.

- Probably the best-known group of religious revivalists within Islam are the various Sufi movements that function in both Sunni and Shiite Islam. Essentially, Sufis are mystics who seek to supplement the strict obedience demanded by the Qur'an and orthodox Muslims with a loving devotion to God. The essence of this movement is the personal quest for spiritual experiences based on a living relationship with God.

- Muhammad: the last and final prophet to whom God revealed his will for mankind in the holy Qur'an, and who now serves as a model and inspiration for all men

- The Five Pillars of Islam: *Shahada*, or the profession of faith; *Salat*, or prayers, which are offered five times a day at fixed hours; *Sawm*, or fasting during daylight hours in the month of Ramadan; *Zakat*, or the giving of alms to the poor, which is similar to what Christians call a tithe; and *Hajj*, the pilgrimage to Mecca mentioned above.

Reflection Questions

1. Whose account of Muslim history does Hexham say is most popularly taught in the West? Why, does he say, is this problematic?

2. Compare and contrast what you've learned of the first one hundred years of Islam's history (after Muhammad's death) with what you've learned of the first one hundred years of Christianity's history (after Christ's ascension).

3. Describe the origins of three different branches/sects of Islam. Where are each of these branches or sects found today, and what has their influence been on Islam as a whole/the Islamic world?

Discussion Question

1. Summarize and describe the origins of Islam.

Quiz

1. According to Muslim tradition, Islam came into existence with the creation of humanity by the creator God known as _____.

   a) Allah
   b) Muhammad
   c) Shiva
   d) Zeus

2. God revealed his will through the first man, Adam, and a long line of prophets including Abraham and Jesus. The last and final prophet was Muhammad (570–632 AD) to whom God revealed the holy _____.

   a) Hadith
   b) Toray
   c) Qur'an
   d) All of the above

3. The angel Gabriel appeared to Muhammad in the lunar month of Ramadan on what is known in Islam as "_____."

   a) The night of truth and grace
   b) The night of excellence
   c) The night of power
   d) The night of power and excellence

4. Muhammad began his preaching in _____.

   a) Jerusalem
   b) Mecca
   c) Baghdad
   d) Cairo

5. (T/F) Shia Muslims represent the majority in Islam.

6. (T/F) According to the majority or Sunni tradition, Muhammad feared the angel who appeared to him was a messenger of Satan and had to be compelled to follow his instructions.

7. (T/F) Zophar is one of the five pillars of Islam.

8. At the Battle of _____ in 624, Muhammad's forces decisively defeated a much larger army from Mecca. This battle was the first clear victory for Muhammad and interpreted as a sign of God's blessing on his divine mission.

   a) Bakri
   b) Baad
   c) Badr
   d) Badq

9. Our knowledge of Muhammad comes not from the Qur'an but from a body of literature known as the_____, a collection of various sayings attributed to Muhammad after his death.

   a) Judith
   b) Hadith
   c) Medina
   d) Caliphs

10. "The Companions" of the Prophet include _____, whom Sunnis claim was the first caliph and the first man to swear allegiance to the Prophet.

   a) Abu Dhabi
   b) Sayyid Qutb
   c) Abu Bakr
   d) Muhammad ibn Abd al-Wahhab

ANSWER KEY

1. A, 2. C, 3. D, 4. B, 5. F, 6. T, 7. F, 8. C, 9. B, 10. C

CHAPTER 24

Muslim Beliefs and Practices

You Should Know

Key Terms

- Sharia law; wahy; ilham; abrogation; jihad

Key Points

- Hexham suggests that Sayyid Abul A'la Mawdudi's 1991 book *Let Us Be Muslims* is an accurate portrait of Islam's traditional teaching regarding the nature of the political state and the necessity of the prevalence of Sharia law therein to accomplish God's purposes.

- Islam is essentially a simple and straightforward system of belief/practice. At its core is the declaration that there is only one true God, Allah, and that Muhammad is his messenger. Implicit in this affirmation is the belief that all other claims to deity, such as those made by Christians concerning Jesus, are false. Islam's basic creed is found in the Qur'an itself, in places such as Sura 57.

- Every true Muslim recites "there is only one God and Muhammad is his prophet" on several occasions daily; the statement is also the basis for conversion to Islam. Muslims also accept the obligations of serving God's law as revealed in the Qur'an and through the life and example of Muhammad as found in the *Hadith*, the records of what the Prophet said and did as an example for all Muslims.

- The ultimate objective of Muslims as God's people is the creation of the rule of God on earth via radical reorganization of human society through religious and moral reform.

- Popular writers in Western societies often argue that the term *jihad* has been misinterpreted by Western writers as a result of what Edward Said called "Orientalism." In their view *jihad* does not mean "holy war"; rather, it means a spiritual struggle. Attractive as this argument is, there appears to be little backing for it in either traditional Muslim texts or the work of more recent writers whose influence shapes modern Islam.

- Sharia law: codified demands of requires submission through the acknowledgment of God's demands laid out in the Qur'an and interpreted by the Hadith, which is believed to be applicable to all people because it enforces morality and God's will on errant humans.

- Wahy: the Muslim understanding of revelation, which claims that Muhammad recited the Qur'an as he received it from God

- Ilham: means approximately what "inspiration" of the Bible has meant in the Christian tradition as taught by traditional Roman Catholics and Protestants like the Princeton theologian B. B. Warfield; literally, "to cause to swallow or gulp down" and is found only once in The Qur'an, in Sura 91:8, which reads: "And inspired it (with conscience of) what is wrong for it and (what is) right for it"

- Abrogation: a doctrine based on Sura 2:106, which reads, "Such of Our revelations as We abrogate or cause to be forgotten, we bring (in place) one better or the like thereof. Knowest thou not that Allah is able to do all things?" Those Muslims who accept the doctrine of abrogation argue that it reflects the power and glory of God, who, in his wisdom, adapted his revelation to changing circumstances and the needs of both individuals and the community as a whole. They also argue that it helps believers explain apparent contradictions in the Qur'an.

- Jihad: holy war and struggle, through which Islamic government and rule is brought

Reflection Questions

1. Based on Muhammad's example, Hexham explains, "Muslims are

committed to a radical reorganization of human society based on the principle of radical religious and moral reform." Contrast this with the Calvinistic theory of "sphere sovereignty" advanced by Abraham Kuyper. What do you find appealing about each philosophy? On what basis does each group believe their philosophy to be the correct one?

2. Explain the difference between *ilham* and *wahy*. Why would it be a mistake to assume that one English word, "revelation," can translate both Arabic terms?

3. How might proponents of "jihad by the sword" explain that it brings freedom? What part does Sharia law play in this liberation?

Discussion Question

1. Summarize and describe the Muslim view of the miracle of the Qur'an. How does the doctrine of abrogation relate Muslim views and interpretation of the Qur'an?

Quiz

1. (T/F) Every true Muslim recites "there is only one God and Muhammad is his son" on several occasions daily.

2. (T/F) The ultimate objective of Muslims as God's people is the creation of the rule of God on earth via radical reorganization of human society through religious and moral reform.

3. (T/F) The Muslim doctrine of ilham is a major source of misunderstanding of Islam in the West.

4. (T/F) The term ilham is much closer to what Christians mean when they speak of the Bible as "inspiration."

5. The doctrine of abrogation
   a) Is entirely rejected by some Muslim scholars who suggest it is the teaching of those who went astray or are actually the enemies of Islam

b) Accepted by the majority of Muslims as a normal part of interpreting the Qur'an with some claiming that hundreds of verses in the Qur'an are abrogated
c) Can be a very confusing doctrine for a non-Muslim
d) All of the above

6. Islam
   a) Rejects the secular Western notion of the separation of religion and morality from the duties of the state
   b) Traditionally allows for no separation of church and state nor is this idea even a remote possibility
   c) Believes the Muslim community is the community of the faithful that submits to God's law as revealed in the *Hadith*
   d) A & B

7. According to Dr. Hexham, jihad is
   a) Misrepresented by popular writers in Western societies who frequently argue that the term "jihad" does not mean "holy war" but, rather, a spiritual struggle
   b) Understood by Sunni and Shiite Muslims to be a means of bringing freedom to all people so that they are free to choose to serve God
   c) Seen by Muslims as providing a practical way of imposing God's law (Sharia) on society to free people from their own evil inclinations and the evils encouraged by rulers who do not acknowledge the true law of God
   d) All of the above

8. Hexham maintains that jihad is indeed primarily a form of warfare waged in defense of Islam, therefore it is highly misleading to dismiss someone like _____ as "extremist" or claim that people like him "don't understand Islam."
   a) Sayyid Qutb
   b) Osama bin Laden
   c) Ayman Al-Zawahri
   d) Hasan al Bann

9. Islam, for Muslims, is a religion of peace in the sense that the imposition of Islamic rule brings areas under Muslim control to peace and order in accordance with Islamic teachings about _____.

  a) The teachings of the Qu'ran
  b) The teachings of Muhammad
  c) The will of Muhammad
  d) The will of God

10. Jakub Zaki taught that "the Conquests" of the first century of the Muslim era as the second greatest miracle of Islam, the first being _____.

  a) The reception of the Qur'an
  b) The reception of Muhammad
  c) The reception of Allah
  d) The reception of Hadith

ANSWER KEY

1. F, 2. T, 3. F, 4. F, 5. D, 6. D, 7. D, 8. B, 9. D, 10. A

CHAPTER 25

Muslim Piety

You Should Know

- Muslim piety is closely related to the Islamic calendar.

- The Islamic calendar differs from Western calendars in following the lunar year while the Western calendar follows the solar year. As a result, although there are twelve months in the Muslim year, an average year has 354 days because the average interval between new moons means lunar months vary between twenty-nine and thirty days in length.

- Because of differences between the solar and lunar years and the prohibition against inserting what might be described as a thirteenth month to create a type of leap year at regular intervals, Muslim calendar months actually move backwards by eleven days each year.

- As a result, the Muslim year works on a thirty-three-year cycle and contains the following months: Muharram; Safar; Rab' I; Rabi' II; Jamadi I; Jamadi II; Rajab; Ramadan; Shawwal; Dhul-Qu'da; Dhul-Hajja.

- Two other things need to be noted when interpreting the Qur'an. First, Muslims clearly distinguish between the early, or Meccan, and the late, or Medinan, Suras. Second, because the historical context of the verses is not clear from the text itself, the meaning of many verses has to be explained from other sources.

- Hegira: the first day of the Muslim calendar, the flight of Muhammad and his followers from Mecca to Medina in September 622

- Ablutions: carefully prescribed acts of cleansing

- Rakahs: a series of ritual actions combining standing, kneeling, standing again, and falling down on one's face while reciting passages from the Qur'an that express praise and adoration of God and submission to him

- Four ways and tools of interpreting the Qur'an: 1) ultimately, the Qur'an itself; 2) example of Muhammad; 3) Imja, or consensus of the Muslim scholarly community; 4) Qiyas, or nalogical argument using deduction and induction based on the other three sources

Reflection Questions

1. Imagine you are a Muslim committed to the rituals that Hexham describes in the sections "Daily Prayer" and "Communal Prayer." How would these commitments change the shape of your days — your schedule, work, and relationships — this week? What challenges might you face in attempting to fulfill these commitments?

2. How would you answer someone who says that "Muslims and Christians all pray, believe in one God, and respect the Bible; there's no difference between religions, anyway"? Respond to each assertion.

3. Compare and contrast Muslim beliefs about the Qur'an's origins and status with Christian beliefs about the Bible's origins and status.

Discussion Question

1. Summarize and explain the four ways in which the Qur'an is interpreted. What are some examples of Qur'anic interpretation? Offer a few from the section in this session.

Quiz

1. (T/F) Muslim piety is very closely related to the pilgrimage.

2. (T/F) Because of differences between the solar and lunar years and the prohibition against inserting what might be described as a

thirteenth month to create a type of leap year at regular intervals, Muslim calendar months actually move backwards by eleven days each year.

3. (T/F) The confession translated "There is no God but Allah. Muhammad is his Prophet" is whispered into a child's ear at birth, forms part of Muslim prayer, and is confessed daily. As such, it is the basis of Islam.

4. (T/F) At each time of prayer throughout the day, Muslim worshipers prepare themselves by carefully prescribed acts of cleansing called ablutions, which are designed to separate themselves from this profane world.

5. Worshipers perform a series of ritual actions called _____: standing, kneeling, standing again, and falling down on one's face while reciting passages from the Qur'an.

   a) Rakahs
   b) Du'a
   c) Hadith
   d) Shahada

6. Personal prayer as most Christians know it does exist in Islam as supplications or _____.

   a) Rakahs
   b) Du'a
   c) Hadith
   d) Shahada

7. Praying to God in the intimate manner of North American evangelicals wherein God is approached as a loving, heavenly father is virtually _____ to pious Muslims.

   a) Blasphemous
   b) Spiritual
   c) Blessed
   d) Personal

8. Muslim prayer is quite different from what most North American Christians and even non-Christians consider prayer. It is, however, similar to acts of prayer found in _____ Christian traditions such as Eastern Orthodoxy and Roman Catholicism.

   a) Liberal
   b) Mainstream
   c) Liturgical
   d) Neo-evangelical

9. Practicing Muslims are commanded to pray ___ times every day.

   a) Six
   b) Eight
   c) Nine
   d) Five

10. Which of the following is *not* one of the five purposes of prayer for Muslims?

    a) To acknowledge servitude to God
    b) To communicate with God in an intimate manner
    c) To be reminded of God's law by reciting the Qur'an
    d) The creation of community

ANSWER KEY

1. F, 2. T, 3. T, 4. T, 5. A, 6. B, 7. A, 8. C, 9. D, 10. B

CHAPTER 26

Sayyid Qutb and the Rebirth of Contemporary Islam

You Should Know

- Based on the Islamic thinking he adopted, Sayyid Qutb viewed Christianity as having been born in a colonial society dominated by Rome and Roman law. As Christianity spread throughout the Roman Empire, it was impossible for Christians to impose their law on the empire.

- Under St. Paul, Christians turned inward, offering a spiritual solution to the world's problems. The Romans were heirs of a pagan culture, but Christians accommodated themselves by proclaiming the separation of church and state.

- To Qutb, the separation of church and state was completely unacceptable; it meant an abdication of responsibility on the part of Christians that allowed paganism to remain triumphant in a Christian society. As a result of the spread of Western European colonial thought, such attitudes had penetrated the Muslim world leading many Muslims to believe such thinking was "scientific."

- Qutb believed an Islamic revolution was necessary to restore Islam to its rightful place in society since life had embraced a blind belief in science and soul-destroying materialism. Man was not worshiping God but materialism, therefore it was the duty of Muslims to preach the law of God and bring all humans into submission to him.

- To do this, Muslims needed to return to God's one true revelation to humankind, the Qur'an, and to the example of the Prophet contained in the *Hadith*. Qutb appealed to the ancient doctrine of abrogation to explain apparent contradictions in the Qur'an and blamed Jews for placing doubts in the minds of Muslims. He taught that although there is no compulsion in religions, the goal of all Muslims is to establish a state guided by God's law where people can freely choose to become Muslims because their natural tendencies to disobey God's laws are restrained by the state. Thus, "no compulsion" does not mean that Muslims cannot use force to establish Islamic rule; on the contrary, jihad is a legitimate means of extending Muslim domain and thus the rule of God's law.

- Assessing Qutb is an exceptionally difficult task. On one hand, it is claimed that his works are intended to build bridges between the Muslim community and the rest of society. Yet, Ayman al-Zawahri (b. 1951), one of the cofounders of Al Qaeda and the man likely to be appointed successor to the late Osama bin Laden (1957–2011), considers himself a disciple of Qutb. Despite the natural tendency to view such zealots as terrorists only, the depth of their religious devotion should not be overlooked; in their minds, they are acting out of personal devotion and piety. Unless we understand this key dynamic, it is impossible to understand the dynamics of militant Islam. Despicable as terrorist actions may be, there is a logic to the actions of groups such as Al Qaeda that is rooted in their particular interpretation of the Qur'an; such interpretation is solidly based in the work of Qutb and similar writers. There can be no doubt regarding the influence of Qutb on the Al Qaeda movement. Finally, there are some remarkable similarities between Qutb's work and the so-called Traditionalist school of writers and thinkers such as Guénon and Schuon who were so concerned to articulate arguments against modernity.

- Although virtually unknown in the West, Sayyid Qutb (1906–1966) is widely recognized as the most influential Muslim writer of the twentieth century. Born in Egypt, he came to see himself as a citizen of a new Islamic civilization he believed represented the wave of the future.

- Sayyid Qutb books/writings are widely read throughout the Muslim world today as the most articulate summation of Sunni Islam in modern times and also among Shia Muslims and other smaller Islamic sects in Iran. Qutb's appeal is his offer of a vision of a new Islamic world within reach yet quite distinct from the corrupting influence of Western culture.

- Qutb came from an old and pious Muslim family of landowners who were experiencing financial difficulties as a result of changing conditions at a time when Egypt was ruled by the British. His birth coincided with the stirring of Egyptian nationalism among the educated and wealthy elite. The nationalism of Mustafa Kamil eventually sought the complete independence of Egypt from foreign control and influences, particularly that of the British, and founded the National Party.

Reflection Questions

1. Qutb's perspective on his experience in the U.S. illustrates the diverse values held by international students spending time in Western nations. Formulate at least three questions you could ask a Muslim international student about his or her perceptions of your own society, of Christianity, and of the relationship between the two.

2. How did Qutb view the separation of religion and state in the West? What, does Hexham say, did Qutb believe were the reasons for the triumph of pagan and materialistic thinking in Western societies?

3. Simply placing the label "liberal," "fundamentalist," or "fanatic" on a person does not explain their actions or the reasoning behind those actions. What labels have others placed on you to avoid having to discuss complex perspectives? What labels have you placed on others? What is a preferable approach, and how would you apply it to understanding, then assessing, the perspectives of Sayyid Qutb?

Discussion Question

1. Who is Sayyid Qutb? Explain in what way he is the most influential Muslim writer of the twentieth century and his relationship with the rebirth of contemporary Islam.

Quiz

1. The junior college attended by Sayyid Qutb:
    a) Sayyid Qutb
    b) Dar al-Ulum
    c) Ayman Al-Zawahri
    d) Hasan al Bann

2. Founded the Muslim Brotherhood in 1926:
    a) Sayyid Qutb
    b) Dar al-Ulum
    c) Ayman Al-Zawahri
    d) Hasan al Bann

3. A modern Muslim terrorist agency:
    a) Al Qaeda
    b) Al Qud
    c) Muslim Brotherhood
    d) Islamic Brotherhood

4. Included Guénon and Schuon who were so concerned to articulate arguments against modernity:
    a) Progressive school of writers/thinkers
    b) Reformed school of writers/thinkers
    c) Democratic school of writers/thinkers
    d) Traditionalist school of writers/thinkers

5. An anticolonial liberation movement that sought to restore Egypt's independence and the dignity of Islam by rooting its politics in Muslim tradition:
    a) Al Qaeda
    b) Al Quda

c) Muslim Brotherhood
d) Islamic Brotherhood

6. His nationalism eventually sought the complete independence of Egypt from foreign control/influences, particularly that of the British, and founded the National Party:
   a) Sayyid Qutb
   b) Mustafa Kamil
   c) Dar al-Ulum
   d) Ayman Al-Zawahri

7. Some believe this one of the most influential books on Muslim belief ever penned:
   a) *Milestones*
   b) *Life and Times of Muhammad*
   c) *In the Shade of the Qur'an*
   d) *Commentary on the Qur'an*

8. An enormous and erudite commentary on the *Qur'an*:
   a) *Milestones*
   b) *Life and Times of Muhammad*
   c) *In the Shade of the Qur'an*
   d) *Commentary on the Qur'an*

9. Widely recognized as the most influential Muslim writer of the twentieth century:
   a) Sayyid Qutb
   b) Dar al-Ulum
   c) Ayman Al-Zawahri
   d) Hasan al Bann

10. One of the cofounders of Al Qaeda and the man likely to be appointed successor to the late Osama bin Laden:
    a) Sayyid Qutb
    b) Dar al-Ulum
    c) Ayman Al-Zawahri
    d) Hasan al Bann

ANSWER KEY

1. B, 2. D, 3. A, 4. D, 5. C, 6. B, 7. A, 8. C, 9. A, 10. C

Notes

www.ingramcontent.com/pod-product-compliance
Lightning Source LLC
LaVergne TN
LVHW030634080426
835508LV00023B/3363